COSMIC MIND, MEDITATION & DNA

PANDIT ATRE

DEDICATION

DEDICATED TO MY THREE GURUS
SATYAM, SHIVAM, SUNDARAM

SATYAM: The first and foremost his holiness Swami Chinmayananda who had left a permanent impression on my mind and guided me in achieving what I am in today's world.

SHIVAM: Shri Rajabhau Gokhale who was responsible in giving philosophical training to me in his day to day dialogues.

SUNDARAM: My departed wife Srimati Kumud Atre who practiced Raj Yoga in her life and was great inspiration to me in finding my path in this material world.

कल्याणप्रार्थना

सर्वेत्र सुखिन: सन्तु सर्वे सन्तु निरामय: ।

सर्वे भद्राणि पश्यन्तु मा कश्चिद दु:खमाप्नुयत् ।।

सर्वस्तरतु दुर्गाणि सर्वो भद्राणि पश्यन्तु ।।

सर्व: सद्बुद्धिमाप्नोतु सर्व: सर्वत्र नन्दतु ।।

दुर्जन: सज्जनो भूयात् सज्जन: शान्तिमाप्नुयात ।।

शान्तो मुच्योत बन्धेभ्यो मुक्तश्चान्यान विमोचयेत ।।

ॐ सहनावक्तु । सह नौ भुनक्तु । सहवीर्यं करवावहै ।।

तेजस्विनावधीमस्तु मा विद्विषावहै ।।

ॐ पूर्णमद: पूर्णमिदं पूर्णात् पुर्णमुदच्यते ।

पूर्णस्य पूर्णमादाय पूर्णमेवावशिष्यते ।।

ॐ शान्ति: शान्ति: शान्ति: ।।

Let all be happy. Let all free from diseases. Let all realize what is good. Let No one subject to misery. Let all be freed from dangers. Let all rejoice everywhere. Let the wicked become virtuous. Let the virtuous attain tranquillity. Let the tranquil be free from bonds. Let the freed make others free.

OM Let Brahman protect us both, the preceptor and the disciple. Let Brahman nourish all of us. Let we all work together with great energy. Let our study be vigorous and fruitful. Let we not hate each other.

Om. Peace, Peace, Peace.

DIALOGUE WITH READER

Dear Readers

This gives me immense pleasure to hand over my fifth book COSMIC MIND, MEDITATION AND DNA to you. As in my previous books my endeavor is to put before you in as simple a language as possible the vedant principles in the light of the present day science. Here I have discussed what cosmic mind is, how it functions and how it is the guiding light of the human mind.

There is an invisible, infinite part of us called the soul. This soul that is Atman is our spiritual core. It is divine spark gifted to us by god and is a part of cosmic primordial energy always present in us. This spark of light called Atman burns brightly within us. In reality it is the essence of who you are and is contained in every breath we take.

As we breathe we must think of life moving in and out of our body. Each of your breathe refreshes and recharges your entire life system. Whenever we feel anxious, fearful or confused a deep breathe taped into the depth of your feelings give you relief. When our body is in a relaxed state every muscle, organ, and fiber of our body gets time to renew and regenerate the tissues and helps the body experience the spiritual vitality that sustains it. And this action is initiated by the primordial vibrations which are synonymous to the sound OM - the Brahm-nad. This Brahma-Nad is also called cosmic mind and is responsible in manifesting innumerable life forms on the earth.

The book also elucidates on the process of meditation which helps the person meditating to calm his mind and concentrate on cosmic consciousness to understand the reality of this mundane material world.

Relaxation is the key to any meditation. It's hard to focus on anything, especially your inner self, when you feel tense or emotionally unbalanced. The quietning of mind is the key to successful mediation. The book deals with process of meditation. The book also discusses how one can effect changes in DNA through deep meditation. Through brain the sound waves which are emanating from cosmic sound tend to interfere with and modify their working much like the interference of electronically charged particles of the solar wind with the radio transmission on earth. Similarly the impulses or electric signals which are given by the brain to other parts of the body through meditation also get affected or modified paving the way to change the damaged strands in the DNA in particular manner. This thesis has support in present modern science as well as Vedant principles nareted by our Rush is and Munees long back when the Vedas were formulated.

I had referred in the Bibliography all the books and and articles which are referred o in this book. But in view of vast amount of literature available it has not been possible to refer to particular passages in the articles and the books in the body of the book. But I want to categorically state that there is no intention to take any credit of opinions expressed by eminent writers whose books find place in Bibliography or even otherwise. All opinions arrived at in this book are mine and I own full responsibility for it.

I sincerely hope that like my previous books the readers will give me full support for the present book also.

I am great full to my publishers Udveli Books and its Proprietor learned Shri Vivek Mehetre and his colleague for bringing out this book in his usual beautiful manner.

-

Pandit Atre

PROLOUGE

There is an invisible, infinite part of us called the soul. The soul is our spiritual core. It is divine spark gifted to us by god and is a part of cosmic primordial energy always present in us. This spark of light called Atman burns brightly within us. In reality it is the essence of who you are and is contained in every breath we take.

As we breathe we must think of life moving in and out of our body. Each of your breathe refreshes and recharges your entire life system. Whenever we feel anxious, fearful or confused a deep breathe taped into the depth of your feelings give you relief. When our body is in a relaxed state every muscle, organ, and fiber of our body gets time to renew and regenerate the tissues and helps the body experience the spiritual vitality that sustains it. Relaxation is the key to any meditation. It's hard to focus on anything, especially your inner self, when you feel tense or emotionally unbalanced.

There is age old practice to gain relaxation tried by sages and yoga followers, even the beginners. Begin with your breathing technique. Once

you are centered in the rhythm of your breath, envision each part of your body, one at a time, starting with your toes. Tighten them and then relax. Then concentrating on your legs and relax them in similar way. Slowly

move up to other parts of the body. Once you get your entire body relaxed state starts your meditation.

It is not necessary to have any particular position or asana to get your body relaxed. They advise lying on plane in virtual dead position, but it is not necessary. Jabalodarsanupanishad (;:,i1o:11ct1⬚itf+⬚) which deal with

various Asanas i.e. positions of the body for meditation after describing every asanas and their benefits lord Dattatraya in canto 3, sloka 13 says

येन केन प्रकारेण सुखं धैर्यं च जायते ।
तत्सुखासनमित्युक्तमशक्तस्ततस्माश्रयेत ॥१३॥

yen ken prakarena sukham dhairyam chajayate 1

tatsukhasanamityuktamasaktasamashrayet 11
Any posture which is comfortable and in which aspirant can maintain his

patience and concentration (without getting physically restless and uneasy) is called sukhasana; literally' the posture of comfort and compatibility. Those Aspirants who are not adept or competent enough to adopt tough posture are advised to sit in any position which is comfortable to them. This is very important aspect to be taken into account. What is important is not the posture but that position which help your mind to settle in calm and quite reflexes. Science of yoga is not a rigorous exercise meant to torture the body in the name of purification or spiritualism. The main thrust is on sincerity, dedication, discipline, diligence and commitment on the part of the aspirant so that the objective of meditation and contemplation is achieved. This is important because comfortable position is key to relaxation of muscles and body. Relaxation is key to any process of meditation. It's hard to focus on anything, especially your inner self when you are tense or emotionally unbalanced. When the body is relaxed one can let go all the stress one is holding in every muscle, organ, and fiber of once entire body. Body gets time to renew and regenerate tissues. Relaxation helps body to tap into the spiritual vitality that sustains it.

Adi Shankaracharya has described the true spirit behind **the Asana that is posture, He says:-**

सुखनैव भवेद्यस्मिन्नजस्त्रं ब्रह्मचिन्तनम् । आसनं तद्विजानीयान्नेतरत् सुखनाशनं ।।११२।।
सिद्धं यत्सर्वभूतादि विश्वाधिष्ठानमव्ययम । यस्मिन्सिध्दा: समाविष्टास्तद्वै सिद्धासनं विदु ।।११३।।

अपरोक्षानुभूति

Sukhnaiva bhveddyasminnjstram brahmchintanam/ asanam tadvijaniyaannetarat sukhasanam II 112/1 Siddham yatsarvbhutadi vishvaadhishshthaamvyayam/ samaavishtastdvai sidddhaasanaam viduah /1113/1

One should know that to be real a posture, in which meditation on the Truth happens spontaneously and unceasingly and not any other that destroys one's happiness. That which is well known as the origin of all beings and support the whole universe , which is immutable and in which the enlightened are completely merged - that is known as Siddhasana. The seat on which we sit and the postures in which we sit are both called asana. The scriptures give us guide lines as to where to sit, on what to sit, how to sit and thereafter what to do in meditation. One should choose a clean and quite place, not too high nor too low or underground (which can

be suffocating). The seat would be uncomfortable act as non-conductor of electricity and protect from dampness'.

शुचौ देशे प्रतिष्ठाप्य स्थिरमासनमात्मन । नात्युच्छितं नातिनीचं चैलजिनकुशोत्तरम ॥११॥

गीता ६, ११

Shuchi deshe pratishthay sthirmasnmatman I natinicham chailajinkushottatam II

      chapter 6 s/oak 11 Bhagvat Gita

In Chapter 6, eleventh sloka of Bhagavad Geeta, Lord Krishna said that' One should have a clean spot and established a firm seat of his own, neither too high nor too low, made of a cloth, a skin and Kusha grass, one over the other.

The aim of Ashtang yoga meditation is not to acquire only strong body physics but to unite your jiva that is mind with cosmic mind which is called and denoted as Atman, the cosmic soul, an Absolute truth. This can be achieved through systematic practice of meditation by reciting any japa like word OM ô€€‡ regularly especially in morning hours of sublime atmosphere.

When one practices meditation for a considerable period of time with reciting mantra OMô€€‡ mentally one would hear ten different sounds as a prelude to get introduced to cosmic sound (primordial sound , an eternal sound the Nadabrahm). This has been described by Hansopnishad as follows.

प्रथमे चिञ्चिणिगात्रं द्वितीये गात्रभञ्जनम् । तृतीये खेदनं याति चतुर्थे कम्पते शरीर: ।।१८।।
पञ्चमे स्रवते तालु षष्ठेमृतनिषेवणर्मं सप्तमे गुढविदन्यानं परा वाचा तथोषट्मे ।।१९।।
अदृश्यं नवमे देहं दिव्यं चक्षुस्तथोमलम । दशमं परमंब्रह्म भवेद्ब्रह्मत्मसम्निधौ ।।२०।।

—हन्सोपनिषद श्लोक १८–२०

Prathame chinchingatram dvitiye gatrabhanjanam/

trtiye khedanam yati chturthe kampate sharirah//18// panchame shravate talu shasthe mrutniveshanam/saptame gudhavidnyanam para vacha tathashtame//19// Adrushyam navame deham divyam chakshustathamalam/

dashamam paramam brahma bhavedbrahmatmasannidhow //20//

As a result of vibration created by reciting this mantra OM ▢ that is NADA one experience ten subtle forms of sound and body experiences, different emotional feelings. These feelings reveal themselves in the form of different body reflexes.

The reflex actions of the muscles are controlled by brain and through the meditation one energize mind through the electric activity of brain to experience ten different sounds.

◆   The first sound creates a tickling sensation.

◆   The second sound creates tense or taut muscles leading to spasms.

◆   The third sound leads to perspiration breaking from the body.

◆   The fourth sound creates tremors in the head.

◆   The fifth sound creates salvia to dribble out of the mouth.

◆   The sixth sound causes a rain of amruta the divine bliss also termed as tears of bliss.

◆   The seventh sound bestows upon the meditator the blessings of being acquainted with the profound and most secret knowledge of Brahman the primordial cosmic energy, the atman as against the mind (jiva).

♦   The eighth sound enables the mediator to speak and understand a mystical language. From here on this is a very sublime stage achieved by very few persons who are on path of spiritual ultimate moksha. He can speak and understand any language and meditate with sublime stage of body.

♦   The ninth sound enables the mediator to make him invisible and acquire what is described as third eye and also acquires divine power of insight and infinite vision. This is the stage acquired by rishis and mahants which common man with no firm resolution can ever achieve.

♦   Finally the tenth sound is the stage of acquiring the transcendental and eclectic knowledge pertaining to the supreme Brahman, the absolute truth. A way to get introduced to sublime presence of Brahman the originator of Vishva the ever present primordial sound of energy.

[These aspects have been described in detail in Nad-Bindu Upanishad of Rig Veda. We will discuss them at a later stage]

The relax actions are controlled by brain. Nerves of the brain are actually an electric circuit consisting of a fine maze of ganglions, nerve fibers and nerve endings much like integrated circuit of computers.

[And these aspects help one to instruct the brain to make subtle changes in what are called strands in DNA of an individual leading to positive changes to nullify the effects of deceases especially of the type of cancer. We will deal with this in detail when we come to that topic in subsequent chapters.]

Through brain these sound waves which are emanating from cosmic sound tend to interfere with and modify their working much like the interference of electronically charged particles of the solar wind with the radio transmission on earth. Similarly the impulses or electric signals which are given by the brain to other parts of the body through meditation also get affected or modified paving the way to change the damaged strands in the DNA in particular manner.

As stated earlier muscles of the body react differently to different frequencies or wavelengths.

तस्मिन्मनो विलीयते मनसि संकल्पविकल्पे दग्धं पुण्यपापे सदाशिव: शक्यात्मा सर्वत्रावस्थित: स्वयंज्योति: शुद्धो बुद्धो नित्यो निरञ्जन: शान्तं प्रकाशत इतिवेदानुवचनं भवतीत्युपनिषत् ।।२१।।   –हंसोपनिशद

Tasminmano viliyate manasi sankalpvikalpe dagdham punyapape sadahivah sarvatravsthitah svayamjyotih shuddho buddho nityo niranjanah shantam prakashanm etivedanuvachanam bhavattyupnishatah /121 /l - hansopanishad/1

When the mind and the heart dissolve and become one with the indescribable fathomless entity (Brahman the Absolute) and lose their independent identity and existence, then all doubts and confusions, all perplexities and consternations that had existed till this time did not happen, collapse into their primary source, the Mana (emotional as well as thinking mind and the sentimental heart) of the meditator.

Once the duel entity mind and heart cease to exist, there is no scope for one to make so many resolves. Have so many desires. Get involved in so many things pertain to this mundane world. The world itself ceases to exist because the existence of the world is due to mind. It is the mind that conceives and then gives this world a shape as well as importance.

Since the mind and heart do not exist, then all the deeds, whether good or bad cease to matter. Such liberated man is called Hans. He is supposed to be personification of Shiva (truth, bliss, auspiciousness, wisdom, enlightenment). The ultimate goal is therefore to become synonymous with one's Atma exhibiting all virtues of Shiva the all-pervading and omnipresent, self-enlightened tranquil Brahman.

In the subsequent chapters we will deal with the cosmic mind, its relation with matter and its deep relationship with DNA.

Chapter 1 Cosmic Mind

To get introduced to cosmic mind one has to follow the process of ascent through meditation which introduces you the pathway of the attainment of the Supreme Spirit in liberation.

To get introduced to cosmic mind one has to follow the process of ascent through meditation which introduces you the pathway of the attainment of the Supreme Spirit in liberation.

इन्द्रियेभ्य: परा ह्यर्था अर्थेभ्य परं मन: ।

मनसस्तु परा बुद्धि: बुद्धेरात्मा महान परा ।।१०।।

महत:परंव्यक्तम् अव्यक्तात् पुरुष: पर: ।

पुरुषान्न परं किञ्चित् सा काष्ठा सा परा गति ।।११।।

कथा उपनिषद । खण्ड १. वल्ली ३ श्लोक १०-११

Indriyebhya: para hayartha, arthebhya param mana: / manasstu para buddhi buddheratma mahan para:/110/1 mahata: param avyaktam, avyaktat puru: ha: para:/ puruh: hanna para: kinchit: sa ka:h:ha, sa para gati /111 II (Katha Upnishad.)

To have the sensation of supreme sublime Brahman (which is referred to as the cosmic mind in modern terminology) it is necessary to train our sense objects through meditation. Unless there are objects, sensation regarding the objects cannot arise. But the cognition of the presence of objects is not merely an activity of the sense organs. There has to be a mind to think this process of sensory cognition. The senses of knowledge are five in number; we see with our eyes, hear with our ears, taste with our tongue, smell with our nostrils, and touch with our fingers or the skin. Each sensation is different from the other-the eyes cannot hear, the ears cannot taste, and so on. There has to be a synthesizing principle in order that one single person may be aware that perception is going on simultaneously through the various senses. We can see and hear and touch and taste all at the same time. This simultaneity of the comprehension of sensations is due to a principle of synthesis, beyond and superior to the sensations themselves. This principle of synthesis is called the mind.

Generally, the mind does the work of indeterminate perception.

Let us take an example: When you walk along the street at sunset or dusk, you see something in front of you. This awareness that there is something in front of you is the work of the mind. The mind says, "Something is there," but it does not say what it is that is there. Mere general, indeterminate awareness of the presence of something is due to the function of the mind, but the determinate perception with a decision as to what that object is, is the function of a higher thing, which is the buddhi, reason, or rationality.

अर्थेभ्य परं मन: । मनसस्तु परा बुद्धि:

Arthebhya param manah | manasastu para buddhi

Above the cognitional process of the knowledge of objects through the sense organs is the mind, and above the mind is the rationality which decides the nature of the situation. From where this rationality come from? Here, consider what exactly the Upanishad means by saying that the mind is superior to the objects and the reason is superior to the mind. Here notice that the objects have to be there prior to the operation of the sense

organs; that is, what is called the substantiality of something independent of the sensation thereof is to be accepted in order that there may be valid cognition of the object. Similarly we must accept that the object should be there. If it is an illusory perception, we do not call it right knowledge. In the same way we must accept the presence of a substance called the object independent of and prior to the activity of sensation, we have to also accept a prior mind independent of and beyond the ordinary cognitional mind.

The mind is responsible to sensitize you about the knowledge of objects. The thoughts of people, the minds of individuals, differ one from the other - I have a mind, you have a mind, everyone has a mind - and these minds of individuals are not uniform in their nature. They have a selfÂ-assertive individuality of their own. My mind can know that you have a mind. How does it happen that my mind becomes conscious that you also have a mind? Is your mind an object of my mind, so that my mental process can regard your mind as existing outside my mind?

The mind or the sensations, in order that they may be aware of an object outside, should accept the operation of a medium between the subjective side and objective side; this is regarded as the superintending medium. In a similar manner, it looks that one mind cannot know another mind unless there is something which is beyond the individual mind. There has to be a mind which connects individual minds.

This superior mind which connects all minds is called the cosmic mind. The cosmic mind is a strange condition which the ordinary mind cannot understand. It is the total apprehension of all cognizable or perceivable things and in this condition of cosmic mental operation, there is no necessity for a connecting link between itself and the objects, because objects get subsumed under the operation of the cosmic mind. That is why the cosmic mind is also omniscient. The individual mind cannot know the truth of the object, or the substantiality, the object as such. The individual mind can gather only information regarding the outer characteristics, or what is called the secondary qualities of the object. The object as such cannot be known by the sensations, but not so is the case with the cosmic mind. There, the objects are subsumed under the cosmic mental operation. The object does not stand outside the cosmic mind.

of you in recognizing the objects.

We have seen above what are mind and its originator cosmic mind.

Meditation principally deals with controlling the mind and therefore considers all the diseases of the mind and the ways in which these can be cured. It examines all the 'impediments' of body and mind which hinder or stop a person from taking up and progressing in meditation technique. It sets out how these impediments can be overcome. It also helps to understand the functioning of the mind: how it reacts to experience and how these reactions in turn influence the mind. Firstly, we need to know what the mind is. All that exists is universal mind, denoted as cosmic mind or Brahman in spiritual text. Brahman or universal soul is made up of individual souls that are mind or jivas and include all the Gods and Goddesses which mankind worships, and also your own Soul. The Soul has the power of seeing. The self within experiences, but does not see, being of the form of matter not Soul.

Matter in respect of living beings includes the self and the inner organ (6-l•·d0h<o1 antahkarana) (brain functioning) which has f.,,,1,1 chitta (consciousness),"¢ buddhi (intellect), ⬚ahamkara (ego) and l=!ttti manas (mind).

Chitta is individual and cosmic consciousness. Individual consciousness, whereby the Self (atman) knows that it exists because it is aware of itself, and cosmic consciousness, of objects held in the mind. Chitta has five states: experienced knowledge, misconception, imagination, deep or dreamless sleep and memory (w=nurpramana, fcrq,w:r viparyaya, ⬚vikalpa, f.lm nidra, ⬚: smrtayah).

Mind is made up of the three gunas of satwa, rajas and tamas and is always in motion. Hence, so long as the mind is not under control, chitta experiences fluctuations. Budd hi, the intelligence of the Self, has the power of knowledge and has will power. It discriminates between right and wrong, and decides what to do.

Manas, the sense-mind, perceives objects and reacts. Mind is a servant, not a master of the self. If the self through its buddhi determines that it would like a woman to think of a man, then this is what the woman's mind will do. The contents of the mind are thoughts, feelings, peace and

This cosmic mind is referred to in this verse of the Upanishad when it says i"-<1c-1-11 ô€€† -qu : buddher atma mahan parah : Above the individual mental operation and the reason is a cosmic principle mahat-tattva.

Your meditational technique takes you gradually from mere sensation of objects to the substantiality of the objects themselves, whereby you do not think the objects, but think with the objects parallel. You befriend the objects, and they set themselves in tune with yourself; and vice versa, you set yourself in tune with the objects, so that the world becomes your friend. In a similar manner, the Upanishad tells us in this verse that the individual mind and the reason have to be transcended in the state of a cosmic rationality, which is the Mahat or the universal buddhi, in which the Ahankara also included. Individual faculties are included and transcended in the cosmic mind, which can also be called the cosmic reason.

In this condition of the mahat-tattva, objects do not merely stand parallel to its operation, but are also not independent of its operation. When the cosmic mind thinks, it thinks the objects also at the same time, whereas in the individual mind, it is different. When one thinks, one does not think the objects also at the same time. The objects stand outside the mind. But in the case of the cosmic mind, it is quite different. When the assertion of the cosmic mind takes place, the world of creation is included in it.

This is achieved through constant meditation. For that your goal is to practice thinking in an impersonal manner. You will then be able to make out any meaning of what is the mahat-tattva or the cosmic mind. Nobody has seen the cosmic mind, and an unseen thing cannot be known, cannot be described, and cannot be understood but experienced through logical thinking.

You cannot know that there is a tree in front of you unless your consciousness, which is operating through your individuality, manifests itself externally in terms of the object outside - namely the tree - and envelops it, and takes its shape so that the consciousness of the shape of the object concerned is communicated to the deciding faculty, the reason inside, and you begin to feel that the tree is here. You accept the knowledge that there is the tree. The Atman, the consciousness, goes out

bliss. What the mind most needs in the short run is relaxation (even more than happiness).

And relaxation is the key to serious meditation. Matter, being:-

1. CRITICAL REALISM

We are going to see shortly how cosmic mind referred as BrahmanÂ-the absolute- the primordial cosmic energy in its prime form get transformed into our material world as we experience through sense organs. Let us first consider theory of critical realism as expounded by the Upanishads.

The theory of critical realism is that the percept of the individual is neutral and the real object presented in experience is different from the percept. The datum in experience through the senses is different in quality and reality from the true object which is in the external universe. There is thus a dualism between the actual percept of the senses and the reality behind the sense-experience. There is what is called the universe of the subject and the universe independent of experience by the individual. Reality is not known through sense-experience. What is known is private to the individuals and what is there in fact in the universe is quite a different thing. Reality, therefore, cannot be known through means possessed by the individual.

2. OBJECTIVE IDEALISM

Objective idealism is an epistemological dualism, and it differs from critical realism in holding that the true object of experience is a Cosmic Mind or Universal Thought. This Universal Mind is independent of individual minds. Empirical perception is the form taken by subjective consciousness, but the reality behind this perception is the cosmic Mind. The nature of the cosmic Mind cannot be known through individual perception. Reality is different from appearance. It is necessary that the individual should expand its consciousness to universality in order that it may be enabled to experience Reality.

COSMIC MIND, THE UNIVERSE AND THE INDIVIDUAL

These considerations lead us to the problem of the relation of cosmic mind, the universe and the individual. It must be remembered at the outset that all processes of reasoning proceed from experience of the individual self. 'I am'-this experience does not require any other proof outside itself. It is self-evident. All proofs are the results of and developments from this indubitable fact. The consciousness of one's existence as an individual at once brings into notion the existence of other individuals in an external universe. 'I am' means 'you also are', i.e., 'the world also is'. The being of the world is the correlative of the existence of "I's individuality. There cannot be a subject without an object of experience. The world is the necessary implication of the individual.

But the position, as it is known to us, of the individual and the world does not explain all matters that arise out of this position. Thinking beings, capable of reflection, become eager to know the relation between the world and the individual. What is the cause of this world? How one is connected with the other things of the world? Questions of this kind crop up in the mind. These questions cannot be answered by anything that is the content of sense-experience. The solution can be arrived at by higher synthesis brought about through the deeper consciousness implied in ordinary experience, the consciousness which becomes the direct experience in such higher contemplations. This is the main object of meditation and practicing Ashtang yoga as we will see later on.

The link between the world and the individual should be either of the nature of the object or of the subject. The objective universe is seen as material, and if this is taken to be the nature of the relation between the world and the individual, it would be another name for another part of the universe. In other words, there would be no such thing as relation. We are made to feel that this relation should be conscious, and yet it cannot be identical with the subjective consciousness. The relation between two things cannot be any of these two things. It must be a third thing. Otherwise there would be no perception of difference. Difference is a third category, and there cannot be knowledge of this difference without an underlying unity between the knower and the known. Absolutely unrelated things cannot become co-relatives of each other. The higher synthesis which is in consciousness should therefore be transcending the empirical

distinction between the subject and the object. The world and the individual should be included in this higher consciousness, and yet, none of these should lose their intrinsic worth in it. If we are able to establish this universal conscious relation between the world and the individual, we have established the existence of cosmic mind. It is the necessary postulate which alone can explain the true nature of the various phenomena of the universe. The order, the system, the regularity and harmony of the universe cannot find an adequate explanation without the admission of this all-comprehending Being, which we term God- that is cosmic mind -the primordial energy vibrations.

It does not matter by what name we refer to it, but it has to be admitted in order that we may be consistent in our explanation of the consistency that is in the universe. Our deepest reality is an irrefutable consciousness, and it asserts itself in eve,y one of our endeavors to give an account of experience, subjective or objective.

Without consciousness, there can neither be a universe nor an individual. Nothing can be, if consciousness is not recognized. All value and existence come to a naught when consciousness is abolished from the field of experience. Supreme Intelligence or Consciousness has to be equated with the Sovereign of the Universe-God that is cosmic mind.

The conception of God in the Upanishads is of special significance. The God of the Upanishads is the ▯-H14ff'-I Anta,yami, the Indwelling Presence in the Universe.

The God or the Ishvara of the Upanishads is the Absolute-Individual, the only Person or Purusha, whose form is all that was, is and will be, who transcends the threefold time and is beyond spatiality and its concomitants. In this concept of god -the cosmic mind- are comprehended the possibilities and the potentialities of all the Jivas; in him are also all the actual forms of the Jivas. He is the main source of knowledge and power. He is omnipresent, omniscient, and omnipotent. He is, to the universe, the highest representative of Satchidananda, Brahman. He is the universe and he is all the individuals. Different from this cosmic mind, there is no universe, no individuals. Ishvara is Brahman from the cosmic standpoint. Brahman is Reality unrelated. As long as the Absolute is experienced as an object by differentiated individuals, it shall appear as a material universe of changing forms, a not-self contending with the self. Differences cannot be annihilated in individualistic perception. Only the Experience-Whole can reveal the reality of the

indivisible Absolute, whose essence and existence is Consciousness, Eternal, without any relation to external appearances.

The Upanishads, it is true, do not give us a systematic account of reality. They are collections of statements of Truth in its various phases. These statements are made not by one but several seers in different Upanishads. We have to study the Upanishads carefully and thoroughly in order to gather a philosophical system from them. It is the genius of Adi Shankaracharya that for the first time evolved a consistent system out of the diverse declarations of the Upanishads. It is the argument of Shankaracharya that reason should not be unbridled, but should conform to the intuition expressed in the Upanishads. Reason can be made use of till its limit is reached, but beyond this limit the Shrutis or the words of the spiritual preceptor alone are the support. Reason has, therefore, a value, but within certain limits Tarka (discussion). And Anubhava (experience), Yukti (reason) and Shruti(revelation), logic and intuition, should go hand in hand. As long as it is possible to make use of the power of reason in determining truth, it is one's duty to use it; but when its limit is reached, it should be abandoned. Any further use of it would lead to error and not truth. We cannot conceive of a greater respecter of reason than Adi Sankarachrya , and yet no one could be more conscious of its defects and limitations. Reason and faith in the intuitional declarations together becomes the royal road to the realization of Brahman. The lower truths are useful until higher truths are realized.

An attempt at attaining to the truth of experience takes us through two ideas-the subjective and the objective. The subjective idea considers things as purely mental or idealistic. The universe, according to it, is an externalized form of mind or idea. But, it will be clear that this is not a tenable position. Experience shows that the object of consciousness is not more real or more unreal than the experiencing idea or consciousness. If the idea of the perceiver is to externalize itself as something in the universe, there must be a basis for it. We have objective perception in dream-experience. We have a dream-space, a dream-time and dream-objects. It may be said that all that we perceive in dream is an idea. But, if we critically examine this position, we shall notice that there is something deeper implied in the argument than what is apparent. What is the meaning of dream? It is known that, in dream-experience, there is a dream-subject together with dream-objects. I become the perceiver of the dream-objects in my dream. But is this dreaming individual identical with

the waking individual?

One becomes a subject in dream; and also is the subject in the waking state. The question that arises here is: Is this dreaming individual who is different from the dream-objects the same as the waking individual who is different from the objects of waking experience? On thinking carefully over the issue, we find that they are different from each other. The waking individual contains within himself the dream-subject as well as the dream-objects. It is the waking subject that has externalized his ideas as the dream-subject and his universe. When we wake up we find that not only the dream-universe is not there, but the dream-subject, also, is not there. The dream-subject and the dream-objects are unified in the waking subject. This gives us a clue to the relation of the individual to the universe. Even as the dream-subject is different from the dream-objects, this waking subject is different from the waking universe; but even as the dream-universe is not created by the dream-subject, so the waking universe is not the product of the waking subject. And, even as the subject and the objects in the dream state are resolved into another subject in the waking state, the waking subject and the waking universe are resolved into another subject which is Purushottama or Vi rat. Ishvara contains in himself all the objects and subjects. The universe is the objectification of the Cosmic or Universal Consciousness, and not of any individual mind.

Ishvara is the Soul of the universe, the Cosmic Self, the Cosmic Mind, who is the efficient and material cause of the individual minds; the individual has no independent existence apart from cosmic mind; it includes in itself both mind and matter. Brahman (the Absolute) is

Ishvara divested of cosmic relations, and Ishvara is Brahman in relation to the cosmos.

When we try to introduce a relation among these principles, i.e., cosmic mind, the universe and the individual, we have already created difference. The difference implied in their conception is the very basis of our processes of thinking. How can we think of the nature of the Divine Being without objectifying it in space? This is why the Upanishads hold that Ultimate Truth is transcendental. The mind of man cannot think of anything independent of objectivity. This is the fundamental error in human perception. Cosmic mind transcends space, time and causation. In order to think of this cosmic mind which we always refer as Godhood, we have to transcend these limiting factors. And we cannot do that. The moment we try to avoid these things, we avoid our own existence. The

thinker ceases to exist in the attempt at transcending relativity of perception and experience.

Philosophy leads us up to a certain stage of thinking; not to the Ultimate Truth. Philosophy trains the intellect in order to recognize its own limitations. It can only make us understand how much we can know in the universe and what we cannot know. The limit of the reasoning power is revealed by philosophy. But the Upanishads do not stop there, with mere reason or with understanding. They reveal the relation among the principles of Godhood, the world and the individual. Only 311ro"⬚cqq Aparoksha-Anubhava, or immediate experience, can reveal the truth of this relation. It is non-relational experience, without a relation between the perceiver and the perceived. It is not like man conceiving of God, but God knowing that he is. 'I am'- this is the knowledge of God. Here differs the knowledge of God from the knowledge of man. Man knows: 'I am; and others also are'. But God's experience is not like that. When He knows, 'I am', nothing else exists. This 'I' includes everything; there is no space, time or causation for Him; it is pure Consciousness.

To us, who think as individuals situated in space, time and causal relations, the Absolute appears as something which must have some kind of connection with the universe of our experience. We take the universe of objective perception for granted, and then argue that there must be an Absolute beyond the universe. We cannot disregard the universe, for we see it before our eyes and experience it; and we cannot also abandon the Absolute, for without it all experience seems to become self-contradictory and meaningless. We have also to retain our own individuality, for we do not see any difference between our being and our individuality.

Now let us consider how this cosmic mind- the absolute Brahman-created the world as we see and live in. One must remember that in every creation there is present a

Nano particle or☐☐ sukshma anurenu of supreme Brahman thus having relationship and control over entire creation, organic and inorganic world as we know. That is why when we meditate we are able to contact this individual soul or jiva and achieve unification with sublime supreme cosmic mind also called 'nadabrahmha'-the primordial energy vibrations ever present in cosmos.

Creation of material world by cosmic mind (Brahman) has been beautifully explained by Mahopnishad. We are going to dwelt upon it instantly. Here we must take into account the wording or terminology used

by the learned seers while expounding the Vedanta principles of one absolute Brahman and its creation into different forms, termed as Nama and Rupa, while giving stress on the principle that there exists only one Brahman, the ever present ☐ nadabrahma the primordial cosmic energy denoted here as cosmic mind.

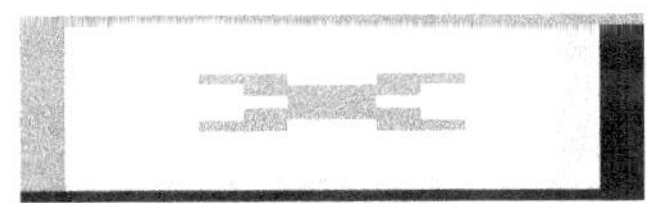

Athato mahopanishadam vyakhyasyamah//1//

tadahureko ha narayana aasinna brahma neshano

napo nagnishomou neme dyavapruthvi n suryo n chandrama //2// s ekaki n ramate //3// Canto 1

Before the world is created there was only a cosmic primordial energy vibrations denoted in our scriptures as Brahman the Absolute. This Brahman which in this chapter we are referring as a cosmic mind is in the form of continuous low density vibrations which gives a sound familiar to Mantra OM □. This energy is the prime conscience. This cosmic mind has its own intelligence which transcends into all forms in material world. So as the Mahopanishad says in the beginning there were no stars, sun, moons other celestial bodies or the material world as we know today. The Brahman felt lonely.

Tasya dhayanangtahsthasya yadnyastommuchyate //4//

tasmin purushachaturdash jayante ekaa kanya dashendriyani mana ekadaham tejo

dvadashoahankarastrayodashakah pranashchyaturdash atma panchadashi buddhi bhutani panchamatrani panch mahbhutani sam ekah panchvimshatih purushah //5//

tatpurusham purusho niveshya nasya
pradhansamvatsara jayante/ sanvatsardhijayante //6//
Canto 1

The supreme Brahman- the cosmic mind to end this
loneliness and initiate the process of creation termed
yadnyastoma that is supreme sacrifice by the Brahman-
the Supreme Being. In the beginning 14 males and
females emerged from cosmic mind. They are
represented symbolically as follows:-

a.   Five organs of perception- nose, tongue, eye,
ear, skin

b.   Five organs of action- hands, legs, mouth,
genitals, excretory

c.   One mind

d.   One Ahankara, (ego, pride, haughtiness,
arrogance, and hypocrisy)

e.   One Prana (the vital wind force that sustains life
in the creature that is breath.)

f.   One Atma (the soul, spirit, pure consciousness,
present in jiva the creature which gives him his own
identity)

g.   Female is Budd hi (intellect and power to
discriminate)

n addition to above five perceptions called tanmatras are smell, taste, sight, hearing, and touch were also created.

The five basic elements earth, water, fire, air and water termed as panch mahabhutas were also created. These five pancha mahabhutas collectively called macrocosmic body of the VIRAT PURUSHA (huge, colossus, all-encompassing form of the first primal male element of creation. The lessor creations emerged from him. In this macrocosmic virat purusha was injected spark of life giving principle. The Supreme Being called Narayan- the cosmic mind- is responsible for creation of various dimensions of time such as past, present and future, as well as years, days, seasons and the various aspects of life cycle.

(All these as we will see in subsequent chapters are coded for posterity in detail in seventh and eighth strands of DNA- the double helix which is the store house of information about emergence of worlds and cosmos, which is not yet completely decoded)

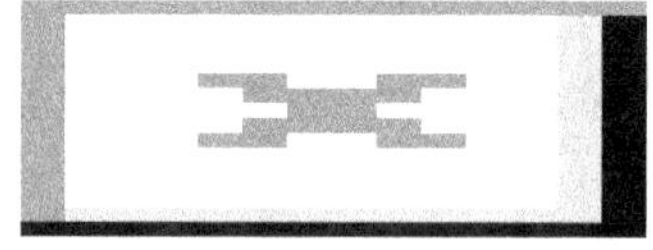

Atha punareva narayanah so'nyatkamo manasa dhyatah
I

tasya dhayananah-sthasya lalatatryakashah shulapanih purusho jayate/ bibhrachriyam yashah satyam brahmcharyam tapo vairagyam mana ashirvayam sapranava

vyahrutayah rugyajuhsamarthvangirasah sarvani chandansi tanayange samashritani/

tasmadishano mahodevo mahadevah//7// Canto1

As a result of meditation by Narayana-cosmic mind- a male was created from his forehead. He had trident in his hand and three eyes, Fame, majesty, glory, truth, self-restraint and continence, austerity, and penances, renunciation and dispassion, accomplishment and successes, all the four Vedas namely Rigveda, Yajurveda, Samaveda and Atharvaveda, all the signs of creation including ever present cosmic NAO referred as OM which represents brahma and all the chandas were represented by this Purusha the one and only one Mahadeva. Having all these elements and virtues established in him he is referred to as Ishana meaning the great lord Mahadeva- the Brahman- the primordial energy itself.

Atha punareva narayanah so'nyatkamo manasa dhyat I

tasya dhyanantahsthasy /alatotsvedaoutpatat I

ta emah pratata aapah/ tatsgtejo hiranyamadam I

tatra brahma chturmukhojatat I Bl I Canto 1 I

Afterwards Narayan- cosmic mind - thought for something and again

mediated. While mediating drops of sweet emerged from his forehead. Those sweat drops spread everywhere like a cloud or vapor of moisture, emerged the first egg-shaped Hiranyagarbha which evolved into four headed Brahma, the god who is said to be Prajapati responsible for creation of different life forms- organic and inorganic. This can also be interpreted that these sweet drops were the primordial fluid forming the cosmic primordial substance which spread the entire Brahmand eventually molding itself to create the all life forms of the world.

(Here we must note that this is electronic event which is responsible in forming the DNA- double helix code in which the entire information of individual life formation as well as events that were responsible for creation of world from its inception were recorded by cosmic mind for posterity)

सोएध्यायत। पुर्वाभिमुखो भूत्वा भूरिति व्याहृतिर्गायत्रं ऋग्वेदोएग्निर्देवता ।
पश्चिमाभिमुखो भूत्वा भुवरिति व्याहृतिस्त्रैष्टभं छन्दो यजुर्वेदो वायुर्देवता ।।
उत्तराभिमुखो भूत्वा स्वरिति व्याहृतिर्जागतं छन्द: सामवेद: सूर्यो देवता ।
दक्षिणाभिमुखो भूत्वा मह इति व्याहृतिरानुष्टुभं छन्दोएथर्ववेद: सोमो देवता ।।९।।

खण्ड १ । महोपनिषद।

Sodhayatl purvabhimukho bhutva bhuriti vyahrutirgayatram hrugvedoagnirdevata/

Pashimabhimukho bhutva bhuvariti vyahrutistraishatabham chando yajurvedo vaurdevata I

uttarabhmukho bhutwa svariti vyahruirjagatam chandah samavedah suryo devatal

daxinabhimukho bhutva maha eti vyahrutiranushtubham chando atharvedah soma devata//9// Canto 1

This Prajapati Brahma turned his face towards east and chanted mantra Bhuah ⸱: from Rig-Veda and created fire God. Then turning his

head to the west he said mantra Bhuvah ⸱: the trishupa chanda, from Yajurveda and the wind god appeared. Next he turned his head to the north and said Svah ⸱:

the Jagati chandas, from samaveda and Created Sun God. Lastly turning to south he mediated upon Mahah, the anushtup chandas and the moon god is created. This sloka narrates how the

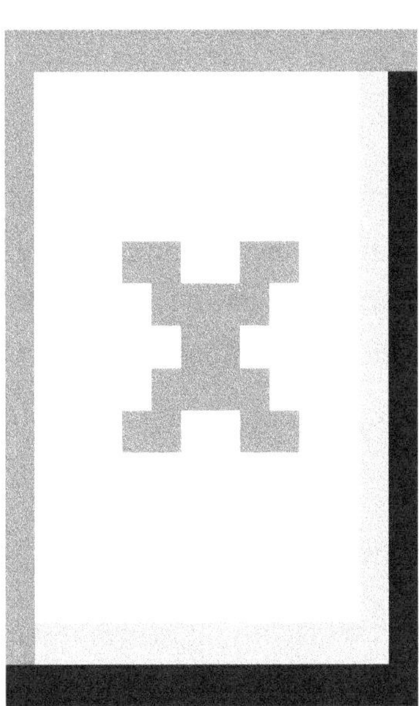

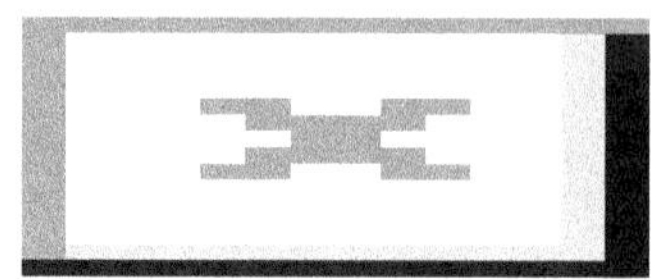

Tadbhamatramidam vishvamiti na syatattah pruthak/ jagadbhedopi tadbhanamiti bhedopi tanmayah In I I savargah sarvasambandho gatyabhavann gachatil nastyasavashrayabhavatsduptvadthasti cha 1181 I vidnyanamanandam brahm raterdatuah prayanaml sarvasankalpsanyasschetasa parigrahah 11911

jagratah pratyayabhavam yasyahuh pratyabhavam yasyahuh

pratyayam budhah I

yatsankochvikasabhyam jagatpralaysrushtyah 111 Oli

nistha vedantvakyanamath vachamgocharah I ahamsachchitparanandbrahmaivasmi na chetarah

//11// canto 2 I Mahopanishad

This Universe is only a reflection of the Atma and hence it is not separate from it. The different worlds that are seen rather different distinctions that appear in the world outside are nothing but the part and parcel of Atma-the cosmic soul. (7).

Since the cosmic soul-the Brahman - is related to all that exists it is present in everywhere. But since it is pervading entire cosmos in reality it is immobile cosmic phenomenon unchangeable. Vedanta calls it Absolute Brahman-the cosmic soul. (8)

It is an embodiment of the supreme bliss and happiness originating from wisdom and enlightenment representing Brahma. It is the ultimate abode of those who do the charity and give donations, alms. When the mind abandons all aspirations, desires, ambitions, determinations, and wishes and hopes it is equivalent to acquiring or accessing Brahman. Because then one obtains permanent peace and tranquility and becomes free from restlessness and agitations (9).

When erudite one says that with the absence of identifying the pure self with external world in the state of existence called 'waking state of consciousness he is experiencing of the Brahman- the cosmic mind- by that enlighten one.(10)

It is the Atma or Brahman that the words of the Vedas express their firm faith, belief, trust and conviction. It is "That" which is beyond the purview of speech. This Brahman is that supreme, truthful, eternal, transcendental and blissful Bramah- the only one and no one else (11) Canto 2 Mahopanishad

To prove our point let us look it from different point of view. Kundikopanishad iifu:scfi1qf.1151e, is the part of Samaveda. It describes the life

period which we denote as 'sanyasashram', 1 ô€€⍰F.Â£tlfllô€€''- Here the Upanishad gives stress on the fact that the Brahman that is cosmic mind and subtle form of that cosmos is the soul that is called Pranava or OM. This in turn is called Akshar Brahma. Sloka 14 of this Upanishad says

'विश्वाय मनुसंयोगं मनसा भावयेत्सुधि: ।
आकशाद्वायुर्वायोज्योतिर्तिज्योतिर्तिष
आपोएदभ्य: पृथिवि । एतेषां भूतानां ब्रह्म पपद्ये ।
अजरममरमक्षरमव्ययं प्रपद्ये ।
मय्यखण्डसुखाम्भोधौ बहुधा विश्वविचय:।
उत्पद्यन्ते विलीयन्ते मायामारुतविभ्रमात ।।१४।।

Vishvaya mnusanyogam manasa bhavayetsudhih/ akashadvayurvajytirtirtisha aapodbhayah pruthvi | etesham bhutanam brahma prapadye | ajarmmrmxaramvyayam prapadye | mayykhandasukhambhodhou bahuda vishvavichayay | uatpadyante viliyante mayamarutvibhramat//14/l

Kundikopanishad, sama veda.

The seeker should be convinced that the cosmic form of Brahma and the subtle form of the soul of that brahma the cosmic mind called Pranava or OM which in turn called Akshar Brahma has a dual meaning. Pranava or Om is called the 'imperishable word' the primordial sound from which the vacha the language emerged. 52 alphabets of Sanskrit are supposed to be the origin of all sounds and languages of the world presently spoken.

The seeker must be aware that wind was produced from the sky, the light i.e. fire from the wind due to friction, water from the fire when it cools down, and earth from the water due to sedimentation and solidification process. These five are therefore called the basic elements or Bhutas, Namely sky, wind, fire, water and earth. The Brahma, the primordial sound, the eternal imperishable cosmic phenomenon pervades uniformly in all these elements and inject the vitality and energy of life in them. Strong winds representing Maya (worldly delusions, ignorance, hallucinations accompanied by attachments and infatuations with this world and their accompanying troubles, torments and miseries) strike the person's mind creating waves which form and dissipate continuously. But these are simply superfluous and transient in nature, they do not represent true form, which is dense, fathomless and un measurable endless energy of bliss and happiness of beatitude and felicity in the form of your atman i.e. soul or enlightened and pure consciousness, the real recognition of cosmic mind which is nothing but supreme bliss.

In furtherance of the above proposition the Mahaopnishad through Janaka's Upadesh describes what is meant by and who is entitled to get it.

इन्द्रियेभ्यः परा ह्यर्था अर्थेभ्य परं मनः ।

मनसस्तु परा बुद्धिः बुद्धेरात्मा महान परा ।।१०।।

महतःपरंव्यक्तम् अव्यक्तात् पुरुषः परः ।

पुरुषान्न परं किञ्चित् सा काष्ठा सा परा गति ।।११।।

कथा उपनिषद । खण्ड १. वल्ली ३ श्लोक १०-११

Srunu tadidanim tvam kathyamanamidam maya/ srishuk dnyanvistaram buddhisarantarntram //36// yadvidnyanatpumanasdyo jivanmukttvamapnuyat//37/f

mahaopanishad canto 2

Janaka says I am going to explain you Sage Sukadeva knowledge about metaphysical matters, theology and spiritualism. once you acquire it you will be close to get liberation and deliverance and emancipation called jivan mukti. The word jivan means life and mukti means freedom and liberation.

यं नास्तीति बोधेन मनसो दृष्यमार्जनम् । संपन्नं चेतदउत्पन्ना परा निर्वाणनिवृत्तिः ।।३८।।
अशेषेण परित्यागो वासनयां य उत्तमः। मोक्षए इत्युच्यते सद्धिः स एव विमलक्रमः ।।३९।।

महोपनिषद खण्ड २ ।

Drushyam nastiti bodhen manaso drushyamarjanaml

sampannam chetdutpanna para nirvannivruttill38ll Asheshen parityago vasanayam ya uttamahl

moxaye etyuchyte saddhiah sa eva vimalkramah

/ /39/ / Mahopanishad canto 21/

Visible world really does not exist. When the mind realizes this fact and believes this firmly it becomes free from the bondage of material objects of the so called visible world. Obtaining this knowledge or realizing it through meditation one gets supreme peace and tranquility symbolizing emancipation and salvation by the realizer.

Abandonment of vasanas that is worldly passions and inherent tendencies that create desires, yearnings, wishes, lust, and attachments towards this world is the best form of emancipation. Learned rishis called this state of renunciation of vasanas equivalent to Moksha.

Drushyam nastiti bodhen manaso drushyamarjanam|
sampannam chetdutpanna para nirvannivrutti||38||
Asheshen parityago vasanayam ya uttamah|
moxaye etyuchyte saddhiah sa eva vimalkramah
||39|| Mahopanishad canto 2||

Visible world really does not exist. When the mind realizes this fact and believes this firmly it becomes free from the bondage of material objects of the so called visible world. Obtaining this knowledge or realizing it through meditation one gets supreme peace and tranquility symbolizing emancipation and salvation by the realizer.

Abandonment of vasanas that is worldly passions and inherent tendencies that create desires, yearnings, wishes, lust, and attachments towards this world is the best form of emancipation. Learned rishis called this state of renunciation of vasanas equivalent to Moksha.

ये शुद्धवासना भूयो न जन्मानर्थभागिनः।

ज्ञातज्ञेयास्त उच्यन्ते जीवमुक्ता महाधियः ।।४०।।

पदार्थभवनादारढ़ायं बन्ध इत्यभिधीयते ।

वासनातानवं ब्रह्मन्मोक्ष् इत्यभिधीयते ।।४१।।

Ye shuddhavasana bhuyo n janmanarthbhaginah |
dnmyatdnyeyast uchyate jivamukta mahadhiyah||40||
padarthabhavanadardhyam bandha etyabhidhiyate |
vasanatanvam brahmamoxa etyabhidhiyate ||41||
Mahopanishad Canto 2||

Only those persons who have good, uncorrupt, untainted, righteous, pure and good vasanas, which are considered good and desirable, those whose life have no distress, miseries, misfortunes, any kind of offence or sorrow in it and those who acquired knowledge of the essence that is worthy to be known are supposed to be fully freed or liberated from this humdrum , mundane and entrapping worldly life and are called jivan mukta. (40)

The erroneous deduction and fallacious belief that material objects have an actual existence is called worldly shackle. On the other hand, the decay and ultimate perishing and total elimination of the vasanas is called moksha. (41)

हर्षामर्षभयक्रोधकाम्कार्पण्यदृष्टिभिः।
न प्यरामृश्यते योऽन्तः स जीवन्मुक्त उच्यते ।।४४।।
अहंकारमयी त्यकत्वा वासनां लीलयैव यः।
तिष्ठति ध्येयसंत्यागी स जीवमुक्त उच्यते ।।४५।। महोपनिषद खण्ड २।

Harshamarshbhayakrodhakamkarpanyadrushibhiahre/

n paramrushyate yo antah s jivanmukta uchyate//44/ /
ahankarmayim tyaktva vasanam lilayaiva yah/

tishati dheyasangati s jivamukta uchyate/145/ /
Mahopanishad canto 2//

Those who are free from feelings such as joys and exhilarations, sorrows and distresses, and consternations, Kama i.e. desires, lust, passions, yearnings and krodha i.e. anger, grief and regret and other worldly faults associated with the mind and heart are deemed to be free from this mundane, artificial and entrapping world.(44)

Those who can easily forsake egoistic vasanas and have holistic reÂ-nunciative approach towards everything pertaining to this world are truly said to be freed or liberated from the material things of this artificial mundane world.

जरामरणमापच्च् राज्यं दरिद्‌यमेव च ।

रम्यमित्येव यो भूङ्कते स जीवन्मुक्ते उच्यते ।।५५ ।।

धर्माधर्मो सुखं दुखं तथा मरणजन्मनी ।

धिया येन सुसंत्यक्तं स जीवन्मुक्त उच्यते ।।५६।। महोपानिषद खण्ड २।।

Jaramaranmapchcha   rajyam   daridryameva   ch   /
ramyamityeva   yo   s   jivamukta   uchyate//551/
dhamadharmo sukham dukham tatha mara-njanmani /
dhiya yen susamtyaktam s jivamukta uchyate//56/ /

Mahopanishad khand 2/

/

Those who remain even, contended, calm, and peaceful even during adversities such as old age , death, troubles and misfortunes or during prosperity as well as during poverty and dearth of even the necessities of life are the persons deemed to be liberated and delivered from the humdrum and artificiality of this world. (55)

The persons who are successful in eliminating from their minds and hearts the distinction between Dharma and Adharma , noble and ignoble, between sukha and dukha, maran and janma i.e. death and birth, are truly liberated souls freed from shackles of this mundane world (56)

क्षणमायाति पातालं क्षणं याति नभ: ।
क्षणं भ्रमति दिक्कुञ्जे तृष्णा हृत्पद्मषट्पदी ।।२४।।
सर्वसंसारदु:खानां तृष्णैका दीर्घदु:खदा ।
अन्त:पुरस्थमपि या योजयत्यतिसंकटे ।।२५।।
तृष्णाविषुचिकामन्त्रश्चिर्न्तात्यागो हि स द्विज ।
स्तोकेनानन्दमायाति स्तोकेनायाति खेदताम् ।।२६।।   महोपानिषद खण्ड ३ ।।

Kshanamayati patalam xanam yati nabhahsthalam/ Kshanam bhramati dikkunje trushna hrutpadmshatpadi/1241/ sarvasansaradukhanam trshnaeka dirghadukhada/ antahpupurasthmapi ya yojayatyatisankate/1251/ Trushnavishuchikamnvrashchintatyago hi s dvij/ stokenananandamayati stokenayati khedatam/1261/

Mahopanishad   Canto 3//

We must note that this Canto 3 stresses, inter-alia that all pleasures and comforts of this world are deceptive and temporary, and to treat the world as truthful is the great error a wise man can ever make. It narrates that Ahankar (false pride, ego, haughtiness, hypocrisy and vanity) and trushna (the different greed, avarice, desires, yearnings, ambitions and thirst for seeking gratification from sensual objects of this world that a person has) as well as lust for women are the main causes for all the miseries, sorrows, troubles and torments that a man is made to suffer in this world and freedom from their clutches is tantamount to liberation and deliverance.

(Here we must note as we shall see in later dialogue that this Ahankar and trushna are responsible in adding to our DNA coded information which person follows in his subsequent births. The meditation in rejecting these thoughts and acquiring pure and trouble free motivation helps in altering our DNA and make our life peaceful and also give our posterity peaceful life free from deceases. Experiments have shown that the mediation techniques preached in Vedic literature helps achieving this. We will deal with this in subsequent chapters)

नास्ति देहसमः शोच्यो नीचो गुणवर्जितः ।।२७।।
कलेवरमहंकारगृहस्थस्य महागृहम ।
लुठत्वभ्येतु वा स्थैर्य किमनेन गुरो मम ।।२८।।   महोपनिषद खण्ड ३ ।।

Nasti dehasamah shochyo nicho gunavarjitah /127//
Kalevarmahankargruhasthsy   mhagruham/
luthatvabhyetu va sthairya kimnen guro mmah/128/1
Mahopanishad canto 3/1

Our body is most lowly, without any worth and there is nothing greater to grieve for or regret and lament for than this body (27)

In this body like dwelling lives the Ahankara- like householder. One should not bother whether this body survives for a long time or is ruined i.e. dies soon (28)

रक्तमांसमयस्यास्य सबाह्याभ्यन्तरे मुने ।
नाशैकधर्मिणो ब्रुहि कैव कायस्थ रम्यता ।।३१।।
तडित्सु शरदभ्रेषु गन्धर्वनगरेषु च ।
स्थैर्य येन विनिर्णीतं स विश्वसितु विग्रहे ।।३२।।   महोपानिषद खण्ड ३ ।।

Raktamansmysyaasya   sbahyaabhyanre   mune/
nashaekdharmino bryhi kaen kayasth ramyata/131 II
Taditsu   sharadbhreshu   gandharvnagareshu   ch/
sthaeryam yen vinirnitam s vishvasitu vigrahe//32/1

Mahopanishad Canto3//

This body is a lump of blood and flesh. How come this body should appear to be beautiful or charming or attractive or pleasant? {All bodies irrespective of their outward appearance are nothing but conglomeration of blood and flesh and nothing else} (31)

If anyone is foolish enough to think that the lightening in a cloud in winter season and a city of Gandharva's (a type of semi-God; celestial musicians) are stable, only he can believe in the stability of this perishable body(32)

Note. The cloud during the winter season is dry, it does not contain rain. So there is no question of there being lightening or thunder in it. Gandharvas are semi -Gods who have no city of their own, for they live in

दासा: पुत्र: स्त्रियश्चैव बान्धवा:सुहृदस्तथा ।
हसन्त्युन्मत्तकमिव नरं वार्धककंम्पितं ।।३५।।
दैन्यमद दोषमयी दीर्घा वर्धते बार्धके स्पृहा ।
सर्वापदामेकसखी ह्यदि दाह्प्रदायिनी ।।३६।।   महोपानिषद खण्ड ३ ।।

Dasah putrah striyashaiva bandhavahsuhrudastha/ hasanthyunmattamiv naram vardhakkampitam/135/

dainyamada doshamayi deergha vardhate vardhake spruha / sarvadpdameksakhi hyadi dahpradayini 1/361/ Mahopanishad canto 31/

During old age, when one starts to shake and tremble like an intoxicated , incoherent man having hallucinations, the servants, sons, daughters, women, kith and kin -all laugh, jeer and sneer at him (35)

During the old age, when the body becomes impotent, decrepit and unable to act as it did when it was young, the various desires, hopes, expectations, yearnings and aspirations increase manifold. The old age is a friendly companion of all troubles and miseries that burn the heart of an old man (36)

क्वचिदा विद्यते यैषा संसारे सुखभवना ।
आयुः स्तम्बमिवासाद्य काल्स्तामपि कृन्तति ।।३७।।
तृणं पांसुं महेन्द्रं च सुवर्ण मेरुसर्षपम् ।
आत्मंभरतिया सर्वमात्मसात्कर्तुमुद्यतः।
कालोऽयं सर्वसंहारी तेनाक्रान्तं जगत्रयम् ।।३८।। महोपनिषद खण्ड ३ ।।

Kvachida vidyate yaisham sansare sukhabhavana / aayuah stambmivaasaadya kalastamapi kruntati 1/371/ trunam paumsum mahendra ch suvarnam merusarshapam / aatmambhartiya sarvamatmsatkartumudyatah/

kaloyam sarvasanhari tenakrantam jagatrayam 1/381/

Wordily people living in this perishable world think for comfort and happiness. After all, where it is? Time (Kala)　　　　　is ticking away continuously

at the age of a man without any let up. The body gradually and imperceptibly decays and becomes weaker by each passing day. Every day our body changes its composition. But people do not realize this (37)

Time is so potent, powerful and mighty that it can convert a reed or particle of sand or dust into Mount Mahendra where the same reed would become a tall tree, while converting huge mountain, such as the golden Sumeru Mountain into mustard seeds. In another words time can do such impossible and apparently insurmountable tasks as converting non entities into colossus figures of great importance and import while reducing those who are famous and big in the present time to non-descript and inconsequential entities at a future date. It has the potential and is capable of destroying everything; it is eager to devour all that exists to fill the hunger of its stomach. All the three worlds celestial, terrestrial and the subterranean are tormented by and frightened by this Kala, the time continuum. (38)

(As we will see later on here we must take into account that in reality all the worldly things are combination of sub atomic particles which are combined through the reaction or will of cosmic mind expressed through DNA- the double helix genetic code constantly adding new information to code to improve or invite new combinations creating new inventions or things such as creating new species or destroying existing ones. Here the meditation comes to our aid in demanding changes in your defective DNA full of damaged code in respect of particular decease. This we will see in subsequent chapters.)

चेतसा संपरित्यज्य सर्वभावात्मभवनाम्। यथा तिष्ठसि त्वं मुकान्धब्धिरोपमः ।।८।।

सर्व प्रशान्तमजमेकमनादिमध्यमाभास्वरं स्वदनमात्रमचैत्यह्म् ।

सर्व प्रशान्तमिति शब्दमयी च दृष्टिर्बाधार्थमेव हि मुधैव तदोमितिम् ।।९।।

महोपानिषद खण्ड ४ ।।

Chetasa samparityajya sarvabhavatmbhavnam /

yatha tishathasi tvam mukandhabidhiropamah/18/1

sarvam prashantamajmekmanadimdhyamabhasvarm svadanmatramchaityachiharam /

sarvam prashantmiti shabdmayi ch drushtirbadharthmeva hi

mudhaiva tadomitim/19/1   mahopanishad Canto 4

When you stop having attachments to or a sense of possession of all

or any of the objects of this world in its totality and live in the world like a blind, dumb or a deaf man, it is only then that it is possible to obtain stature of a man who remains detached from worldly attachments and withdraw from the notion of "I am doing",. One is then in stance of sarva tyag sanyasa equivalent to Samadhi. Here he experiences Kaivalya leading to supreme bliss. (8)

One must have undeniable conviction that everything visible is "one", is uniform, unchangeable, calm and pacific, and is without a birth, a beginning and a middle and it can only be experienced. All that is visible is a manifestation of the vibrations of thought (enunciated or helped by cosmic mind) having their origin in once own mind. Everything that is felt experienced by mind is one or other form of that singular, non-dual, nonÂ-distinguishable, immutable, unequivocal and immaculate entity called atman (part and parcel of that primordial cosmic energy pronounced as OM and Adi-shakti Narayani)

It is also termed in this Upanishad as Brahman. All the manifestations you see or experienced in reality is non-dual energy termed as Brahman. (9)

दिशोऽपि न ही दृष्यन्ते देशोऽप्यन्योपदेशकृत ।
शैला अपि विशीर्यन्ते शीर्यन्ते तारका अपि ।।४९।।
शुष्यन्त्यपि समुद्राश्च ध्रुवोप्यध्रुवजीवन:।
सिद्धा अपि विनश्यन्ति जिर्यन्तो दानवादय:।।५०।।   महोपनिषद खण्ड ।।३।।

Dishopi na hi drushyante deshopyanyopdeshkrut / shaila api vishryante shiryante taraka api //49// shshyanytyapi samudrashch dhruvopyadhruvajivanah/ siddha api vinashyanti jiryanto dandanavah//50/1 Mhaopanishad Canto 3//

This world is transient and perishable with change in times. Nothing is steady or permanent. Impossible things may happen and things that appear to be happening might actually turn out as impossible. Even the compass fails to show direction during a severe sandstorm in a desert in night. The countries and civilizations perish and become matter of history and remains only in memory. Mountains split and reduced to rubble in a matter of seconds. Stars disintegrate and become black holes in the cosmos. Established ascetics and hermits are crushed. They might die or will overcome by evil forces and lose their stature and holiness. Even one time strong demons overcome by old age and loss their vigor and power. (49-50)

परमेष्ठ्यपि निष्ठावान्हीयते हरिप्यज: ।
भावोऽप्यभावमायाति जीर्यन्ते वै दीगिश्चरा: ।।५१।।
ब्रह्मा विष्णुश्च रुद्रश्च सर्वा वा भूतजातय: ।
नाशमेवानुधावन्ति सलिलानीव वाडवम् ।।५२।।   महोपानिषद खण्ड ३ ।।

Paramehtyapi nishthavaanhiyate haripyajah / bhavopyabhavamayati jiryante vai digishcharah /15/1 brahma vishnuishch rudrashch sarva va bhutajatayah/ nashamevaanudhavayanti slilaniva vaadavam//52//

Mahaopanishad Canto 3/1

Even the grandfather Brahma, the Prajapati, who lives for a very long time and lord Vishnu who has no birth as such, also vanish into oblivion one day, when the time comes for their end. (Here one must recall that Vedas do claim that there are thousands of earths in this cosmos and every earth like planet has its cosmic duration having their own trinity to govern their respective worlds. Each of these worlds is in existence till it is turned into black hole or destroyed by collision with another star or planet. It is in this sense it is said that Brahma and Vishnu are perishable when their time comes).

Abundance turn into shortages, even the patron Gods of the various directions are subjected to old age, decay and death (51)

Great Gods and the whole crowd of creatures are rushing constantly towards destruction even as the water of the ocean heaves and swirls towards the legendary fire called "Vadva" present in the bed of the ocean. (Vadava is a ferocious fire burning in the bosom of earth- a chemical reaction such as split of nitrogen molecules producing energy which is lava in side deep in the core of earth, This fire keeps water of the sea warm and sustains marine creatures , both flora and fauna. This helps in protecting complete eco-system underneath the glaciers and cold and frigid surface of the ocean bed.).॥52॥

यानि दू:खानि या तृष्णा दु:सह्य ये दु:सह्य ये दुराधय: ।
शान्तचेत:सु तत्सर्वं तमोऽर्केष्विव नश्यति ।।२९।।
मातरिय परं यान्ति विषमाणि मृदूनि च ।
विश्वासमिह भूतानि सर्वाणि शमशालिनी ।।३०।।   महोपानिषद खण्ड ४ ।।

Yani dukhani yaa trushna dusahya ye duradhayahl shantchetah su

tatsarvam tamorkeshivava nashyati 112911 matariya param yaanti vishamaani mruduni chal vishavsmiha bhutani sarvani shamshalini 113011 Mahopanishad canto I 1411 Mahopanishad canto 411

In these slokas Mahopanishad Further explains that all the torments, sorrows, anguish and tribulations (duhkh), all the yearnings, desires, avarice and thirst for the world (trushna), and all the insurmountable worries and miseries of a man who has a peaceful, calm and tranquil temperament of the mind and a stable and focused intellect are eliminated even as darkness is removed by the sunlight. (29)

In this perishable and mortal world, a man who has control over his mind is respected and trusted by men of both stern and harsh temperaments as well as by those who are sweet and mild, just like a son believes, trusts and relies upon his mother (30)

Note:- And here comes the importance of deep heartfelt meditation which helps one overcome the attraction towards this unrealistic worldly appearance and pleasures and obtain peace and tranquility the stage of sat-chit-anand, a supreme bliss - step to climb final step of moksha.

संतोषामृतापानेन ये शान्तास्तुप्तिमागता: ।
आत्मारामा महात्मनस्ते महापदमागता: ।।३५।।
अप्राप्तं हि परित्यज्य संप्राप्ते समतां गत: ।
अदृष्टखेदाखेदो य: सन्तुष्ट इति कथ्यते ।।३६।। महोपनिषद खण्ड ४।।

antoshamrutapanen ye shantastuptimaagtaah /

aatmarama mahatmmanaste mahapadmagatah/135//
apraptam parityajya samprapte samatam gtah/

adryshta eside in the khsdakhedo yah santushat iti kathyate//36/

Mahopanishad Canto4//

Those who drink the nectar termed santosh that is which tasted the contentment and satisfaction and feel fulfilled are comforted by whatever they get and remain calm and tranquil, only such wise, sagacious and adroit persons can reside in the Atma and attain the supreme state of pure consciousness (35)

He who doesn't worry about or desire for things that cannot be obtained and instead remains satisfied with whatever has been obtained by him , does not perceive ,feel or pay attention to either comfort or Pain only he is said to be fully and truly contended. (36).

Nabhinandtyasamprapatam   praptam   bhunkte
yathepsitam / yah sa soumya samacharah santushat iti
kthayte   /137/1   ramate   dhiryataprapyate
sadhvivaantaahpurajire /

sa jivanmuktatadodeti savarupaanandday ini /138/1

Mahopanishad Canto4//

He who never unduly expects or gets upset at anything
that has been obtained or received and uses that which
is available to him according to his necessity and needs,
he who acts with equanimity and equity, remains even,
sober and uniform in his behavior with others under all
circumstances such person is considered excellent and
contended in all respects (37)

Just like loyal wife remains happy and contended inside
the householders yard without complaining about any
and everything, when mind of the person remains
contended and satisfied and he feels always contended

and comfortable then this state of mind is called liberated from the shackles of this deluding artificial world. This state of mind is obtainable while the person still leaves in this world and continues to do worldly chores; this state is called "Jivan mukti". It bestows the bliss and happiness of recognizing the nature of the conscious pure-self which is supreme blessedness and happiness personified (38).

शुद्धसन्मात्रसंवित्ते: स्वरूपान्न चलन्ति ये ।
रागद्वेशादयो भावास्तेषां नाऽत्वसंभाव: ।।३।।
य: स्वरूपरिभ्रंशश्चैत्यार्थे चितिमज्जनम् ।
एतास्मादपरो मोहो न भूतो न भविष्यति ।।४।।   महोपानिषद खण्ड ५ ।।

Shuddhsanmmtrasanvite svarupaanna chalitanti ye/ ragdveshadayo bhaavastesham naadnyatvasambhavah /13/1 yah varuparibhranshshachaityarthe citimajjanam / atasmadparo moho na bhavishyanti /15/1 Mahopanishad Canto 5/1

The Atma /soul should be recognized as being pure, uncorrupt and the only authoritative entity which is self-enlightened. Who wizened to this absolute truth and do not distract from their firm conviction about it or have any kind of doubt of it and do not waiver from this firm belief are not affected at all by various faults such as rag-dvesh (anger and hatred, envy and jealousy, malice and ill will and enmity) associated with adnyanam i.e. ignorance. (3)

When the mind- intellect combination diverts its attention from the pure entity

called Atma and plunges or focuses it on the various desires, worldly comforts, pleasures, passions it is submerged in worldly things , it is said to be engulfed in Moha also called Moha-Maya.(4)

(Note.-Here the cosmic mind comes into play in catalyzing different forms which are desired by individual intelligence. Here the person can through meditation control individual intellect and get help form cosmic mind in salvation and emancipation)

सर्व शान्तं निरालम्बं योमस्थं शाश्वतं शिवम् ।
अनामयमनाभासनामकमकारणम् ।।४५।।
न सन्नासन्न मध्यं तं न सर्वमेव च ।
मनोवचोभिरग्राह्यां पूर्णात्पुर्ण सुखात्सुखम् ।।४६।।
असन्वेदनमाशान्तमात्मवेदनमाततम् ।
सत्ता सर्वपदार्थानां नान्या संवेद्नाद्रुते ।।४७।।   महोपानिषद खण्ड ५ ।।

Sarvam shantam niralambam yomstham shashavatam shivam / anamaymanaabhasnaamkaranam /145/1

na sannasann madhyam tam na sarvameva ch / manovachobhrgrahyam purnatpuranam sukhashukham /146/1 Asanvedanmashantamatmavedanamaatatam/

satta sarvapadarthanam naanya sanvedanaadrute/147/1

In verse 38 Canto 4 above we had seen that when mind of the person remains contended and satisfied and he feels always contended and comfortable then this state of mind is called liberated from the shackles of this deluding artificial world. This state of mind is obtainable while the person still leaves in this world and continues to do worldly chores; this

state is called "Jivan mukti". It bestows the bliss and happiness of recognizing the nature of the conscious pure-self which is supreme blessedness and happiness personified (38).

Here verses 45 to 4 ?further explain the matter.

Absolutely calm, tranquil and peaceful, coming into existence without any reason or cause, having no support or prop for its existence and having a form like that of the sky or space, also being eternal, infinite, absolute and universal, and auspicious, truth and beauty. Having no short comings and blemishes, beyond perceptions, imaginations and conceptions and beyond description, attributes and comprehensions requiring no cause or reason for what it is (45). It is neither true nor false, is inaccessible by the mind and speech, beyond the purview of the faculty of speech and the powers of the brain. More complete than simply 'full' and provider or bestowed of the greatest happiness and bliss (46). It is beyond the reach of emotions and sentiments, being peaceful, calm, tranquil and placid, an embodiment or a personification of pure consciousness, all pervading, omnipresent and all encompassing-all these inter alia are the attributes and qualities of the ambiguous Brahma. All these various objects in this world have their existence or rather they derive their importance, significance and majesty due to the emotions and conceptions of the Atma.

In other words the Atma, with the connivance of individual intelligence gives the shape or importance to the objects of the world it comes in contact. If Atma decides so the objects, no matter how alluring and attractive, will lose their significance and importance, allurement and beauty. (47) Here again meditation gains importance in rejecting these allurements and driving individual intelligence in rejecting them as not a reality and correct the mind intelligence calling help from cosmic mind in rejecting false notions of any conceptions about a disease in particular inviting corrections in DNA code for the present and possibly future generation.

Note: From references from Bhagavat Purana-cosmological interpretation of it- we can follow how a transformation from five basic elements called Pancha Mahabhutas to physical entity occurs. The Bhagavatam

(Verses 3-26, 34 - 49) presents an account of Sankhya philosophy, in which the elements of gross matter (air, fire, water and earth) are described as successive transformations of the ether. The

sequence of transformation is as follows:

Sound-ether- touch- air- form- fire- taste-water-odor-earth.

Each element is regarded as the previous element plus an additional property contributed by a subtle sense element (tanmatra). Since the elements are derived from modes of sense perception, they appear to be, in a sense, insubstantial and to be ultimately based on consciousness. Thus from this Puranic perspective, the idea of decoupling an object from other matter and moving it through the ether is much plausible than it is from the standpoint of modern thinking. Here the mind intelligence and its power comes into play and therefore here is the importance of deep mediation directed to transform the defaulting defects in double helix code(DNA) for removing to the extent possible and correct it. In Bhagavatam verse 11.15.21 a form of mystic changes is described based on the mind's power by Lord Krishna.

'The yogi who completely absorbs his mind in Me, and who then makes use of the wind that follows the mind to absorb the material body in Me, obtains through the potency of meditation on Me, the mystic perfection by which his body immediately follows his mind wherever he goes. That is to say, he can rearrange the molecules of the physical body effecting corrections.'

This makes sense from the perspective of Sankhya philosophy, in which the body is a transformation of subtle sense objects connected with the mind. In this transformation air (wind) is the second gross element, after ether.

Note: According to text 21.84 of the Madhya-Lila section of Chaitanya Charitamruta Krishna said to Brahma

"Your universe extends to four billion miles; therefore it is the smallest of all the universes. Consequently you have only four heads."

This suggests that in Vedic times and in subsequent literature we had a concept of many Brahmands (Anant koti Brahmands).

In times of India, Tuesday November 21, 2017, appeared a report giving information about recent scientific invention. Aliens (bugs containing biogenic life forms as microorganisms which travel on space dust to earth and might have been responsible in emerging the life on our planet. Likewise microorganisms from our planet might have travelled on space dust on other planets and stars in our galaxy and forming life patterns there. According to British Scientists powerful flows of interplanetary dust that can travel through space up to 70 km per second.

They further observed that small bio-particles floating at an altitude of 150 km or more could be knocked free of the earth's gravity by incoming space dust. Eventually the tiny organisms could reach other planets in the solar system. Some bacteria, plants and even hardy micro-animals called tardigrades are known to be capable of surviving in space. The same process could occur in reverse, bringing extraterrestrial bugs to earth and possibly helping to seed life on the planet earth. The propositions could propel organisms over enormous distances between planets raises some exciting prospects of how life and the atmospheres of planets originated. The streamlining of fast space dust is found throughout planetary systems and could be a common factor in proliferating life. This process of play of microorganisms and sub atomic particles is referred to as the play of cosmic mind.]

जडतां वर्जयित्वैकां शिलाया हृदयं हि तत् ।
अमनस्कस्वरूपं यत्तन्मयो भव सर्वदा ।
चित्तं दूरे परित्यज्य योऽसि स्थिरो भव ।।५१।।
पूर्वं मन: समुदितं परमात्मतत्वात्तेनाततं जगदिदं सविकल्पजालम् ।
शून्येन शुन्यपि विप्र यथाम्ब्रेण नीलत्वमुल्लसति चारूतरा- भिधानम् ।।५२।।

महोपानिषद खण्ड ५।।

Jada tam varjyitvaikaam shilaya hrudayam hi tat/ amanasksvarupam yattanmayo bhava sarvada 1/51 ll

purvam manah samuditam paramaatvaatenatatam /

shunyena shunyapi vipra yathambrena nilatatvamullsati charutara-bhidhanam/1521/ Mahopanishad Canto 5//

Perversion, turpitude or grossness is the state when the heart is like a stone, while being indifferent or dispassionate and detached towards the world is the state which is obtained when perversion, turpitude or grossness are abandoned. This latter state is desirable and acceptable against the former. One must get established in this state which is without any perversion, turpitude or grossness (51)

In the beginning, the mind was the first creation by the supreme being (cosmic mind). After that, from the mind was created this huge web-like deluding world of confusions, ambiguity, errors and uncertainties. Nothing can be produced or created theoretically from nothing, such as for

example the sky is a blank, deep fathomless void but the various colors of spectacular shades and hues such as blue, violet etc. emerge in it, rather created in this otherwise neutral, blank and actually colorless void of the sky because of the reflection of the sun light from dust particles, moisture and impurities present in the sky. (52). Here what is stressed is that there must be some reason or cause for anything to happen. Since this is a fact that the creation has come into existence, it naturally follows that there must be something which has created it. It may not be apparent or tangible, but nevertheless it is there even as the colors in the sky appear because of the scattering of the sunlight due to dust particles or moisture present in the otherwise apparently clean looking atmosphere. Another interpretation can be given that one mirage leads to another, one erroneous conception about this world sets off a chain of misconceptions in the wake, and one gets sucked in it, going further away from his original setting or moorings or truthful place where he had stood. The blank sky when cloudless appears blue. Setting sun changes its colors to orange or red. In reality sky has no color at all and whatever it assumes or appears to have are due to physical phenomenon of the scattering of sunlight at different angles from the viewer due to dust particles and air molecules present in the atmosphere. We now know beyond the atmosphere of the earth the space extending to millions of light years is colorless blank void.

संकल्पसंक्षयवशाद्गलिते तु चित्तेसंसारमोहमिहिका गलिता भवन्ति ।
स्वच्छं विभाति शरदीव खमागतायां चिन्मात्रमेकमजमाद्यमनन्तमन्तः ।।५३।।

Sankalpsanxyvshadgalite   tu   chittesansarmohmihikaa galita bhavanti/

savachchham vibhati sharadiv khamaagtamtayam chinmaatramekamjmaadyaymanantamntah 1/531/

When 'sankalpa, meaning different volitions, determination, vows and promises, ambitions and aspirations of a person are extinguished, all the inherent tendencies of the mind to yearn for and desire for comfort and pleasures are also dissolved. When this happens the fog or curtain of delusion called 'Maha' is also dispelled, vanished. The only entity that remains is the spectacular Brahma who is akin to the spotless, clean sky at the onset of the winter season and who has the attribute ,inter alia, of being unborn, without a beginning, eternal, infinite and the only one who is an embodiment of cosmic consciousness- the primordial cosmic mind ever present in its non-perishable form.

अकर्तुमकमरङ्गम् च गगने चित्रमुत्थितम् ।
अद्रष्ट्रकं स्वानुभवमनिद्रस्वप्नदर्शनम् ।।५४।।
साक्षिभुते समे स्वच्छे निर्विकल्पे चिदात्मनि ।
निरिच्छंप्रतिबिम्बन्ति जगन्ति मुकुरे यथा ।।५५।।

Akartumkamarangam ch gagane chitramutthitam / adrashatakam svanubhavam Nidrasvapnadarshanam / /541/ saxibhute same svachche nirvikalpe chidatmani / nirichcham pratibimbanti jaganti mukure yatha 1/551/

Mahopanishad Canto 5//

The sky appears as a gloriously, spectacularly and colorfully painted canvas even though there is no painter or color to paint it so beautifully. It has made its appearance like a dream (an illusion) while one is sleeping. It does not bother or wait whether there is anyone observing it or not. It appears whether there is any body to view it or not. (54)

The Atman is pure consciousness, eternal, a witness to all, full of equanimity, is pure, and spotless, without any alternatives, or delusions and it is like a mirror in which all the three worlds (past, present and the future, including celestial, terrestrial and the subterranean , gross, subtle and casual worlds) are reflected without any distortion.

The colors of the sky are optical illusions due to different factors. They appear in the sky due to these factors irrespective of there is anybody to see them. That is they are independent of one's will or efforts. A phenomenon occurred due to play of particles reflecting the sun light as a play of self-asserted reaction. We can say that it is independent of individual volition. The comparison here of the Atma with the mirror is important in the context of it being a witness to all that happening. A witness is not a participant of in any event; he remains a mute spectator, as it were. Mirror while reflecting the images does not participate in any manner; it is mute spectator and reproduce image as it occur. The Atma likewise witness the whole cosmic drama played by cosmic mind without getting involved in it by slightest way.

एकं ब्रह्म चिदाकाशं सर्वात्मकं खण्डितम् ।
इति भावय यत्नेन चेतश्चाञ्चल्यशान्तये ।।५६।।
रेखोपरेखावलिता यथैका पीवरी शिला ।
तथा त्रैलोक्यवलितं ब्रह्मैकमिह दृश्यताम् ।।५७।।

Akam brahm chidakasham sarvatmakam khanditam /

iti bhavay yatnen chetashchaanchalyashantaye /156/1
rekhoparekhavlita yathaika pivari shi/a /

tatha trailokyavalitam brahmaikammiha drushyatam/157/1

Mahopanishad Canto 5//

We had seen time and again that according to Vedanta there is only one permanent thing that is primordial cosmic energy- referred to as Adi-shakti or cosmic consciousness - one and none other. Here in this shloka this is reiterated.

Brahma (the cosmic macro consciousness of the universe) in our chapter referred to as the cosmic mind, is one and the only one reality. It embodies all forms of existence, is all pervading, immanent and omnipresent. It is un-fractional and immutable like the eternal and infinite sky- the space beyond our imagination, fathomless. We have to make diligent efforts to absorb and understand this universal truth in order to calm down the restlessness of our mind (56)

One must visualize the three worlds in Brahma just like lines and cross lines (various contours, engravings, granulations and other physical markings) that are present in big stone (57). The markings on any big stone are part of the natural characteristic feature of that stone giving the stone its intrinsic quality, value and structure. It cannot be segregated from that stone. In a like manner it is not possible to separate Brahma from the myriad variety of the creative world because it is an integral part of the Brahma.

नास्तमेति न चोदेति नोत्तिष्ठति न तिष्ठति ।
न च याति न चायाति न च नेह न चेह चित् ।।१०२।।
सैषा चिदमलाकारा निर्विकल्पा निरास्पदा ।।१०३।।   महोपानिषद खण्ड ५ ।।

Nastameti na chodeti notishthatti na tishatati/ na cha yati na chayati na cha neha na cheha chatll10211 saisha chidamalakara nirvikalpa niraspada II 10311

Mahaopanishada Canto 5/1

The pure consciousness or the Atma has an eternal and stable existence. It neither rises nor ever sets like sun rise or sun set. This pure consciousness is free from birth and death. It neither stands nor remains sitting as it has no physical form. It is neither here nor there but everywhere that is every form or manifestation. (102). This ambiguous Atma which is eternal, enlightened and pure consciousness has no support or foundation on which it rests. It does not need any support to make its existence possible. It is without a second or parallel, and is without any confusions or delusions, errors or uncertainties. It is an immaculate image of epitome of purity and clarity. (103).This concept can be easily understood by taking the example of air. Air has no form of its own. It takes shape of the container in which it is confined. As soon as the container is destroyed or vanished air amalgamates into air outside. Air here is prana because it infuses life into any inner element that is body of a creature and makes it into living being. Without Prana (or ATMA) the body will be of no use. It would be dead and will have no consciousness.

केचिदर्केन्दुवरुणास्त्र्यक्षाधोक्षजपद्मजाः ।
केचिद्ब्राह्मणभूपालवैश्यशूद्रगणाः स्तिथाः ।। १३९ ।।
केचित्तृणौषधिवृक्षफलमूलपतङ्गकाः केचित्कदम्बजम्बिरसालतालतमालकाः ।। १४० ।।
केचिन्महेन्द्रमलयसह्यामन्दरमेरतः । केचित्क्षारोदधिक्षीरघृतेक्षुजलराशयः ।। १४१ ।।

महोपनिषद खण्ड ५ ।।

Kechdakenduvarunasatrayaxadhoxjapadmjah/ kechidbrahmanabhupalvaishyashudraganah sthitaah II 13911 kechirunoushadhivruxflmulpatpatangakah/ kechitkadambjambirsaltalamalatmalakahII 14011 Kechinmahendramlysahyamandrmevah/ kechtixaroddadhixiraghrutexujalrashyah II 141 II

Mahopanishad Canto 5/1

These verses describe rather elaborate the cosmic mind's display in manifestation of different physiological forms. The Atma, a part and parcel of cosmic primordial energy- the cosmic mind- takes many forms in this

world. Some of them have assumed the form of Sun and Moon, while others have assumed Varuna (the water God) Hari (Vishnu-the sustainer and protector), Shiva - the annihilator or concluder- and Brahma - the patriarch of creation .(139).

(Here we must take into account the Vedic concept of many worlds - anant koti Brahmands, Here narration relates to one brahmand which should apply to other bramhands also.)

Some have become Brahmans, while others have Kshatriyas, Shudras etc. It also takes form of herbs, twigs, grass, reeds, trees, fruits, roots, and leaves. While some takes the form of lemons, Kadambas (the neculea Cadamba tree), mangoes, coconuts, tobacco plants.(140)

The Atma also take forms of rocks, boulders, stones, and pebbles, mountains like Mahendra, Malaya, Saya, Mandara, Meru etc., (these are old names prevalent at the time of Upanishad was formulated. In the current period we can refer to Himalayas, Sahyadri, Alps, Silicon Valley etc.)

There are many manifestations which are assumed by Cosmic mind such as ocean, milk, clarified butter, sugar cane juice, and various water bodies, Rivulets, rivers and lakes etc. (141)

केचिद्द्विशाला: ककुभ: केचिन्नद्यो महारथा: ।
विहरन्त्युच्चकै: केचिन्निपतन्त्युत्पतन्ति च ।।१४२।।
कन्दुका ईव हस्तेन मृत्युनाऽविरतं हता: ।
भुक्त्वा जन्मसहस्त्राणि भूय: संसारसंकटे ।।१४३।।
पतन्ति केचिदबुधा: संप्राप्यापि विवेकताम् ।
दिक्कालाद्यनवच्छिन्नमात्मतत्वं स्वशक्तित: ।।१४४।।
लीलयैव यदादत्ते दिक्कालकलितं वपु: ।
तदेव जीवपर्यायवासनावेशत: परम् ।।१४५।।
मन: संपद्यते लोलं कलनाकलनोन्मुखम् ।
कलयन्ति मन:शक्तिरादौ भावयति क्षणात् ।।१४६।।
आकाशभावनामच्छां शब्दबिजरसोन्मुखीम् ।
ततस्तद्घनतां यातं घनस्पन्दक्रमान्मन: ।।१४७।।
भावयत्यनिलस्पन्दं स्पर्शबीजरसोन्मुखम् ।
ताभ्यामाकाशवाताभ्यां दृढाभ्यासवशात्तत: ।।१४८।।

महोपानिषद खण्ड ।।५।।

\

develops various sankalpas that is hopes, desires and determinations to acquire those objects of this materialistic artificial world (180). With these desires relevant actions are initiated by the creature to fulfill them. These actions soon get a momentum like speeding vehicle. But these are causes of various sorrows and miseries but never happiness, peace and tranquility

(181).

Therefore one should diligently and sincerely try to stop the process of creation of various sankalpas arising in the one's mind. He must never be lured by the materialistic world of artificiality. By constant indifference these sankalpas gradually destroyed and die similarly as sprout of the seed dies if it does not find proper nourishment and conducive environment (182).

[Note.- Here again one should remember the cosmic mind plays a role through volitions of your individual mind and provides help in getting nearer to salvation. Here comes the importance of mediation in steading your mind and rejecting various sankalpas to clear it of illusions which are materialistic world. Next verses 183 and 184 explain it beyond any doubt]

भावनाऽभावमात्रेण संकल्प: क्षीयते स्वयम् ।
संकल्पेनैव संकल्पं मनसैव मनो मुने ।।१८३।।
छित्वा स्वात्मनि तिष्ठ त्वं किमेतावति दुष्करम्। यथैवेदं नभ:
शून्यं जगच्छुन्यं तथैव हि ।।१८४।।   महोपानिषद खण्ड ५ ।।

Bhavana bhavamatren sankalpah xiyate svayam / sankalpnaiv Sankalpam manasaiva mano mune/ / 183/ / chchitva savatmani itshath tvam kimetaavati dushkaram/ yathaivedam nabhah shun yam jagachchunyam tathaiv hi /1184/ /

Mahopanishad canto 5/1

In the absence of any fanciful ideas in the mind with regard to this world, the various sankalpas that is volitions, ambitions, desires automatically on their own come to an end. Therefore firm determination and resolve of the intellect to trounce worldly attractions is very necessary. This requires strong will power to control the mischievous mind. This can be achieved through the intellect.(183).

One should therefore firmly establish and revert to his pure self. He should realize true nature of his real and pure Atma and stop playing with

this deluding, corrupt, deceptive artificial world which is devoid of any substance. Its real nature is just like the void of the deep sky. (184).

Tandulasya yatha charma yatha tamrasya kalmia I nashyati kriyayaa vipra purushasya tatha ma/am I I 185I I tandulsyeva ma/am sahajampya/am I

nashyatyev n sandehstsmaaduyogvanbhavet I I 186I I

Mahopanishad canto 5//

In the concluding verses of canto 5 (khanda5) it is advised that even the reddish taint of copper (formed by the oxidation of copper) and husk of the rice grain can be removed by diligent efforts and industry using proper means, likewise the various faults, flaws and blemishes of a person can be removed by making sincere and diligent efforts (185)

[Note: here it must be noted that the meditating and concentrating on the removal of notions about particular illness comes within the definition of sincere and diligent efforts to get free from the clutches of that illness.]

Just like grain of rice or wheat is covered by a shell of chaff or husk, a person is surrounded by various faults and shortcomings (such as notion of particular illness) . But still due diligence, sincere effort and industry it is possible to destroy them. Hence one should be firmly rooted in once truthful nature, which is the pure, uncorrupt, eternally conscious Atman. Therefore one should be diligent, committed in his spiritual pursuits. There is nothing such as impossible or being impractical in it. (186).

खेदोल्लासविलासेषु स्वात्मकतृर्ततयैकया ।
स्वसंकल्पे क्षयं याते समतैवावशिष्यते ।।३।।
समता सर्वभावेषु यासौ सत्यपरा स्थितिः ।
तस्यामवस्थितं चित्तं न भूयो जन्मभाग्भवेत ।।४।। महोपानिषद खण्ड ६।।

Khedillavilaseu svaatmkarturtatyaikyaa / svasankalpe xayam yaate samataivavshishyate 1/31/ samata sarvabhaveshu yasou satyapara sthitihi / tasyamavsthitam chittam n bhuyo janmbhagbhavet 1/41/

Mahopanishad Canto 6/1

Man himself creates sorrows, anguish, troubles, joys, happiness, exhilarations, cheerfulness and pleasant circumstances. When all sankalpas (volitions) are removed or annihilated only uniformity of emotions, equanimity and even mindedness remains. A person does not see any difference between pleasant and unpleasant circumstances. (3). When a person firmly establishes uniformity of approach in his dealings with the worldly affairs and when he treats equally all material things, then he gathers real sense of equanimity and uniform and universal approach towards material things of the world it is only then the cycle of transmigration comes to an end.(4) .

हृदयात्संपरित्यज्य सर्ववासनपङ्क्तयः ।
यस्तिष्ठति गतव्यग्रः स मुक्तः परमेश्र्वर : ।।८।।
दृष्टम् द्रष्टव्यमखिलं भ्रान्तं भ्रान्त्या दिशो दश ।
युक्त्या वै चरतो ज्ञस्य संसारो गोष्पदाकृति ।।९।।
सबाह्याभ्यन्तरे देहे ह्याध ऊर्ध्व च दिक्षु च ।
इत आत्मा ततोऽप्यात्मा नास्त्यनात्ममयं जगत ।।१०।।

Hrudayatsanprityajya sarvavaasanapanktyaah / yaastishatati gatavyagrah s muktah parmeshchar I/BI/ drushatam drashatvyamkhilam bhranta bhrantya disho dash/ yuktya vai charato dnyasya sansaro goshpadakruti 1/91/ sabahyabhayntare dehe hyadh urdhvam ch dixu ch/

ita aatma tatoopyatma nastyanatmmaya jagat/11 DI/

Mahopanishad Canto 6//

[Note:- These verses again stress the importance of not to fell in the trap of vasanas, volitions, desires, pleasant and unpleasant and concentrate on pure nature of atman, the sub particle of cosmic mind that is Adishakti - primordial cosmic energy which engross the entire cosmos and which is indivisible, one and only one reality. Here once again the stress must be given to deep mediation which unable one to realize the truth.]

Now turning to verbal translation, those who remove or eliminate their vasanas that is inherent tendencies to be attracted towards the world, from their hearts are truly liberated and freed and they become peaceful and tranquil. They are like the supreme lord or the most exalted soul of creation called Parmeshwara.(8). Such people are deemed to have seen all the illusionary and deceptive images of things present in the world that has to be seen by them while wandering in all directions of the world. For an erudite and enlightened person, his diligent efforts to understand the truth in the correct directions renders the world as insignificant and inconsequential, meaningless and easy to cross as the depression made on earth by hooves of a cow. (9).

The Atma is present everywhere-inside and outside our body, above and below it in every direction uniformly and universally. For an enlightened and erudite person this world can never be without the Atma. It can never be devoid of Atma. World and Atma both are complimentary to each other. (10).

सर्वं समतया बुध्या यः कृत्वा वासनाक्षयम्।
जहाति निर्ममो देहं नेयोऽसौ सनाक्षयः।।४४।।
अहंकारमयीं त्यक्त्वा वासनां लिलयैव यः।
तिष्ठति ध्येयसंत्यागी स जीवन्मुक्त उच्यते ।।४५।।
निर्मूलं कलनां त्यक्त्वा वासनां यः शमं गतः।
दूनेयं त्यागमिमं विद्धि मुक्तं तं ब्राह्मनणोत्तमम् ।।४६।।   महोपानिषद खण्ड ६।।

Sarvam samataya budhya yah krutva vasanaxayam / jahati nirmamo deham neyosou vasanaxayah 1/441/ Ahankarmayim tyaktva vaasanam lilyaiv yah / tishathati bheyasangati sa jivamukta uchyate 1/451/ nimulam kalanam tyaktva vasanam yah shamam gatah/ dneyam tyagmimam vidhdi muktam tam brahmanottamam /1461/ Mahapanishad Canto 61/

A person who uses his stable and equitable mind to forsake "vasanas" permanently and becomes dispassionate and detached from this world of sensual objects only succeeds in breaking free from all shackles associated with the gross body and the sensual world. Abandonment of vasanas is the supreme necessity for spiritual aspirants. (44) .. Those who honorably and with comfort without any compulsion and use of force forsake and abandon pursuing all egoistic yearnings and desires are

called "Jivan mukta. A person who is Jivan mukta, while still leaving in this artificial world even though detached from bondages leads a normal, active life out worldly but inwardly he is complete neutral and not affected by anything he does. (45).

(Note: Here I want to add that there is compulsion for seekers of jivan mukti to abandon the desires for worldly pleasures through the deep meditation as is advised by the Vedanta philosophy of Astanga Yoga sadhana. This we will touch in next chapter in detail.)

Persons who let go their Vasanas which are image of the various sankalpas that they have from their root such persons achieve great spiritual and moral powers. This renunciation towards the worldly objects of such persons is worthy of praise and being emulated. This is because they had reached the stage where they have realized the essence of supreme reality of the cosmos (46).

आपादमस्तकमहं मातापितृविनिर्मितः ।
इत्येको निश्चयो ब्रह्मन्बन्धायासविलोकनात् ।।५५।।
अतीतः सर्वभावेभ्यो वालग्रादप्यहं तनुः ।
इति द्वितीयो मोक्षाय निश्चयो जायते सताम् ।।५६।।
जगज्जालपदार्थात्मा सर्व एवाह्मक्षयः ।
तृतीयो निश्चयश्चोक्तो मोक्षायैव द्विजोत्तम ।।५७।।   महोपानिषद खण्ड ६ ।।

Apadmastkamham matapitruvinirmitah /

ityeko nishchayo brahmanbandhayasviloknaat 1/551/
atitah sarvebhyo valgradpyaham tanuah /

iti dvitiyo moxaya nishchayo jayate satam//56// jagajjalpdarthatma sarva evahamxyah /

trutiyo nishchoukto moxayaiv dvijottam //57//

Mahopanishad Canto 6//

In these verses categories or types of faith, conviction and belief are discussed. The first is that "my whole body from the leg to the head is a result of conjugal relationship between my parents". This body is falsely recognized as once real body. But this is not. This is a product of the relationship of my parents. It is not eternal, neither it is imperishable and will decay and perish one day. (55). The second one is that the sorrows in

the shackles or fetters that tie the person to the world is tantamount to they being put in the captivity of his mind and subjected to submission to mind's falls notions of worldly attractions.(56). The third conviction is that "I am the essential being or life called the conscious Atma of all the animate as well as the inanimate world. I am an image of the cosmos-cosmic mind-and am imperishable. This third conviction is the sound basis for one's Mukti. Here he realizes his true identity as the Atma also called soul. (57).

Once you stopped about thinking about this world and unnecessarily bothering yourself in what is good and what is bad and concentrate on the work in hand and do it dispassionately not being attached emotionally to the results, you acquire gracious and compassionate heart for everyone. You then have attained the supreme peace and tranquility. This supreme bliss will make you calm and peaceful and part of the great ocean where there is no turmoil, no huge waves or whirlpools to cause any kind of consternation and torments to your mind. There is only supreme bliss called sachchidand-eternal calmness.

शून्यं तत्प्रकृतिर्माया ब्रह्मविज्ञानमित्यपि।
शिवः पुरुष ईशानो नित्यमात्मेति कथ्यते।।६१।।
द्वैताद्वैतसमुद्भुतैर्जगन्निर्माणलीलया ।
परमात्ममयी शक्तिरद्वैतैव विजृम्भते ।।६२।।
सर्वातीतपदालम्बी परिपूर्णैकचिन्मयः ।
नोद्वेगी न च तुष्टात्मा संसारे नावसीदति ।।६३।। महोपानिषद खण्ड ६।।

Shunyam tatprakrutirmaya brahmvidnyanmityapi / shivah purush eshno nityamatmeti kathyate//61 II dvaitadvaitsamudbhtairjgnnirmanalilaya/ parmatmamyi shaktirdvaitaiv vijrumbhatc/162// sarvatitpadalmbi paripumaaikchinmayah / nodvegi n ch tushtatma sansare navsidati//63//

Mahopanishad Canto 6//

The phenomenon known as Atma has a number of synonyms such as void that is a state of nothingness symbolized by sky or space element, infinite, measureless, eternal, spotless, clean and uncorrupt. It is in this void Brahma resides. Maya denotes delusions, deceptions, hallucinations, ignorance, as well as the cosmic creativity. Prakruti stands

for nature with its stupendous powers. Brahma dnyana denotes knowledge of the transcendental entity which is supreme and absolute-metaphysics and spiritualism. Purusha is described as the first male, the primordial male aspect of nature and also macrocosmic Vi rat Purusha of or Vishnu. Ishana- the lord Shiva, Lord of all God and everything else- the symbol of or insignia of auspiciousness, divinity, righteousness, wisdom and enlightenment personified. 61). The non-dual, transcendental and supreme consciousness is the stupendously powerful energy that has manifested itself as both the non-dual and dual aspects of the creation as well as the various material objects needed for its construction, development, progress, sustenance and enhancement. (62). Those people who take shelter of the supreme, transcendental state which is beyond the reach of the entrapping net cast by the delusions and deception of this world, which is complete and pure consciousness, do not indulge in making efforts in this world and neither they feel satisfied with such efforts. As a result they are never subjected to sorrow and torments of the visual but artificial world as seen by them in the waking state of consciousness called Jagruta. (63).

Note:- Here we must take note that the persons who acquired the status of jivan mukta as seen by us in previous verses realize the true function of the Supreme energy - the Adi-shakti- . In its play of dual manifestation it assumes different forms and also necessary forms for their material growth, stay and decay and are able to denounce them. This they achieve through deep meditation. At this stage the cosmic mind takes over the function of the individual's mind and he assumes his final destination of the jeevan mukti.

प्रशान्तकलनारम्यं नीरागं पदमाश्रय।

एषा ब्राह्मी स्थिथि: स्वच्छा निष्कामा विगतामया ।।७३।।

आदाय विहरन्नेवं संकटेषु न मुह्यति। वैराग्येणाथ शास्त्रेण महत्वादिगुणैरपि ।।७४।।

यत्संकल्पहरार्थं तत्स्वयमेवोन्नयन्मन:। वैराग्यात्पुर्णतामेति मनो नाशवशानुगम्।।७५।।

आशया रक्ततामेति शरदीव सरोऽमलम्। तमेव भुक्तिविरसं व्यापरौघं पुन: पुन: ।।७६।।

दिवसे-दिवसे कुर्वन्प्राज्ञ: कस्मान्न लज्जते।

चिच्चैत्यकलितो बन्धस्तन्मुक्तौ मुक्तिरुच्यते।।७७।।

Prashantklnnrmyam niragam padmashraya /

esha brahmi shthithiah svachcha nishkaama vigatamaya 1/731/

aday vihrnnevam sankateshu n muhyati /

vairagyenath shastren mhtvaadigunairpi /17 4/1 yatsanklphrartham tatsvayamevonnynmannah / vairagyatpurntameti mano nashvshangam/175/1 aashaya rakttameti shardiv saromalam /

tamev bhuktivirasam vyaparougham punah punah /176/1 divase-divase kurvanpradnyaah kasmann lajjate / chichchaitykalito bandhastnmuktou muktiruchayate /177/1

A person who has achieved the status of jivan mukta adopt a pleasant and charming stance free of all attachments of this world and that is freedom from all sankalpas- volitions, ambitions, determinations, vows and promises. This stance- that is way of living- leads him to the state of existence here called as Brahmi. It is accepted as the equivalent of status of Brahma. It means pure, selfless, faultless and devoid of all delusions, deceptions that are associated with the artificial and mundane world. (73). A person gaining the above status does not get deluded even in the adverse circumstances. Both by acquisition of knowledge through the study of scripture and through sincere natural born instinctive renunciation as well as through acquisition of great noble virtues the various sankalpas are completely destroyed and eliminated from his mind which gets elevated to higher level of peace and tranquility.(75).

But mind which seems to achieve fulfillment through renunciation under forces of compulsion or conditions of hopelessness do not achieve stability because when hopes revive and circumstances become favorable, one's mind again becomes like an enchanting, clear and beautiful lake during the winter which attracts person with its charms and cause restlessness in him. This astonishes that when the mind has detached itself and turned away from all relations and attractions again comes back in the daily routine involving the business of worldly affairs. Interaction or contact of the mind with sensual objects of the material world is called shackles or fetters that ties person to this world. (Examples galore in Purana of Rushis and Munies of the caliber and status of Vishvamitra are involved with sensual relationship with Apsaras like Menaka).

To be freed from that unfortunate development and be liberated from that finally is called liberation and deliverance, emancipation and salvation (that is moksha) for the person (76-77) .

चिदचैत्या किलात्मेति सर्वसिद्धान्तसंग्रह: ।
एतन्निश्चयमादाय विलोकय धियेद्धया ।।७८।।
स्वयमेवात्मनात्मानन्दं पदमाप्यसि।
चिदहं चिदिमे लोकाश्चिदाशाश्चिदिमा: प्रजा:।।७९।।
दृश्यदर्शननिर्मुक्त: केवलामलरूपवान्।
नित्योदितो निराभासो द्रष्टा साक्षी चिदात्मक: ।।८०।।   महोपनिषद खण्ड ६।।

Chidchaitya   kilatmeti   sarvasiddhantsangrahah   /
etannishchaymaday   Vilokay   dhiyeddhaya   /178/1
svaynevatmnatmanandam padmapyasi /

Chidaham   chidimelokashchidashashchidimah
prajah/179/1   drushyadarshannirmuktah

kevalamlrupvan / nityodito nirabhaso drashta saxi chidatmakah /180/1

mahopanishad Canto 6//

We had seen above that in understanding the manifestation of cosmic mind in material or physical forms is through coagulation with individual mind also called heart. This recognition comes from deep meditation and following the methods for that given in scriptures.

Here in these verses it is observed that the mind - intellect complex freed from the attractions of the objects of this materialistic world of sensual pleasures is equivalent to the exalted Atma. This is the essence of all tenets of Vedanta. Considering this tenet as the truth and having firm belief in it, one must observe or experience that his pure-self residing in his heart, by the light of illuminated wisdom and intellect. (78) [Albeit through deep meditation].

This will give a person unlimited and extreme bliss, happiness, and joy. He must think that 'I am an image and an embodiment of pure consciousness and reflect and radiate that pure consciousness. He should think that the entire world is nothing but pure consciousness. All the directions, creatures (and things in this material world) are nothing else but pure consciousness.'(79).

When a person distance himself from the object of sight (of this world) and freeing himself from the actual process or efforts of seeing this world

and effort made for that purpose, his Atma becomes a mere witness to what is happening around it. It remains neutral, dispassionate and disinterested observer without being affected or influenced by anything that happening around it. His Atma does not get involved in that happening. (80).

So this is the ultimate truth that awakened Atma of a person who acquired salvation or jivan mukti as seen in the aforesaid paragraphs. Now what is required to understand is how this sublime status is acquired by the enlightened person. Herein comes the importance of following the path of spiritual efforts to be made by a person seeking salvation and achive the status of jivan mukta, a sublime state where nothing else but sublime bliss, the status of sat-chitt-anand is obtained- the eternal peace beyond which nothing remains to be achieved.

This we will discuss at length in the next Chapter 'Meditation'.

CHAPTER-II   Meditation

We, in this Chapter, will discuss the importance of meditation in our desire to achieve the jivan mukti which we acquainted ourselves in the previous Chapter

There is an invisible, infinite part of us called the soul. The soul is our spiritual core. It is divine spark gifted to us by god and is a part of cosmic primordial energy always present in us. This spark of light called Atman burns brightly within us. In reality it is the essence of who you are and is contained in every breath we take. As we breathe we must think of life moving in and out of our body. Each of your breathe refreshes and recharges your entire life system. Whenever we feel anxious, fearful or confused a deep breathe taped into the depth of your feelings give you relief. When our body is in a relaxed state every

muscle, organ and fiber of our body gets time to renew and regenerate the tissues and helps the body experience the spiritual vitality that sustains it.

Relaxation is the key to any meditation. It's hard to focus on anything, especially your inner self, when you feel tense or emotionally unbalanced. There is age old practice to gain relaxation tried by sages and yoga followers, even the beginners. Begin with your breathing technique. Once you are centered in the rhythm of your breath, envision each part of your body, one at a time, starting with your toes. Tighten them and then relax. Then concentrating on your legs and relax them in similar way. Slowly move up to other parts of the body. Once you get your entire body relaxed state starts your meditation.

We had touched this topic in the Prologue but for detail consideration and proper understanding we are repeating it here as it is all important an aspect to be discussed.

It is not necessary to have any particular position or asana to get your body relaxed. They advise lying on plane in virtual dead position but it is not necessary.

Jabalodarsan upanishad ('311?1(11c;?f+aqf.l151c;) which deal with various asanas i.e. positions of the body for meditation after describing every asanas and their benefits lord Dattatraya in canto 3, verse 13 says

येन केन प्रकारेण सुखं धैर्यं च जायते ।

तत्सुखासनमित्युक्तमशक्तस्ततस्माश्रयेत ।।१३।।

yen ken prakarena sukham dhairyam chajayate tatsukhasanamityuktamasaktasamashrayet

Any posture which is comfortable and in which aspirant can maintain his patience and concentration (without getting physically restless and uneasy) is called sukhasana; literally' the posture of comfort and compatibility. Those Aspirants who are not adept or competent enough to adopt tough posture are advised to sit in any position which is comfortable to them.

This is very important aspect to be taken into account. What is important is not the posture but that position which help your mind to settle in calm and quite reflexes. Science of yoga is not a rigorous exercise meant to torture the body in the name of purification or spiritualism. The main thrust is on sincerity, dedication, discipline, diligence and commitment on the part of the aspirant so that the objective of meditation and contemplation is achieved. This is important because comfortable position is key to relaxation of muscles and body. Relaxation is key to any process of meditation. It's hard to focus on anything, especially your inner self when you are tense or emotionally unbalanced. When the body is relaxed one can let go all the stress one is holding in every muscle, organ, and fiber of once entire body. Body gets time to renew and regenerate tissues. Relaxation helps body to tap into the spiritual vitality that sustains it.

Adi Shankaracharya has described the true spirit behind the Asana that is posture, He says:-

सुखनैव भवेद्द्यस्मिन्नजस्त्रं ब्रह्मचिन्तनम् । आसनं तद्विजानीयान्नेतरत् सुखनाशनं ।।११२।।
सिद्धं यत्सर्वभूतादि विश्वाधिष्ठानमव्ययम ।
यस्मिन्सिद्धा: समविष्टास्तद्वै सिद्धासनं विदु ।।११३।। अपरोक्षानुभूति
शुचौ देशे प्रतिष्ठाप्य स्थिरमासनमात्मन । नात्युच्छितं नातिनीचं चैलजिनकुशोत्तरम ।।११।।

गीता ६, ११

In eleventh sloka of Bhagavat Geeta Lord Krishna said that 'One should have a clean spot and established a firm seat of his own, neither too high nor too low, made of a cloth, a skin and Kusha grass, one over the other.

The aim of Ashtang yoga meditation is not to acquire only strong body physics but to unite your jiva that is mind with cosmic mind which is called and denoted as Atman, the cosmic soul, an Absolute truth. This can be achieved through systematic practice of meditation by reciting any japa like word OM 3}, regularly especially in morning hours of sublime atmosphere.

When one practices meditation for a considerable period of time with reciting mantra OM 3}, mentally one would hear ten different sounds as a prelude to get introduced to cosmic sound (primordial sound , an eternal sound the Nadabrahm) This has been described by "Hansopnishad as follows.

प्रथमे चिञ्चिणिगात्रं द्वितीये गात्रभञ्जनम् ।
तृतीये खेदनं याति चतुर्थे कम्पते शरीरः ।।१८।।
पञ्चमे स्रवते तालु षष्ठेऽमृतनिषेवणम ।
सप्तमे गुढविदन्यानं परा वाचा तथाऽष्टमे ।।१९।।
अदृश्यं नवमे देहं दिव्यं चक्षुस्तथाऽमलम ।
दशमं परमंब्रह्म भवेद्ब्रह्यत्मसन्निधौ ।।२०।।   हन्सोपनिषद श्लोक १८-२०

Prathame chinchingatram dvitiye gatrabhanjanam/ trtiye khedanam yati chturthe kampate sharirah//18//

panchame shravate talu shasthe mrutniveshanam/saptame gudhavidnyanam para vacha tathashtame//19//

Adrushyam navame deham divyam chakshustathamalam/ dashamam paramam brahma bhavedbrahmatmasannidhow//20// Hansopanishad.

As a result of vibration created by reciting this mantra OM D that is NADA one experience ten subtle forms of sound and body experiences, different emotional feelings. These feelings reveal themselves in the form of different body reflexes.

The reflex actions of the muscles are controlled by brain and through the meditation one energize mind through the electric activity of brain to experience ten different sounds.

The first sound creates a tickling sensation.

The second sound creates tense or taut muscles leading to spasms. The third sound leads to perspiration breaking from the body.

The fourth sound creates tremors in the head.

The fifth sound creates salvia to dribble out of the mouth.

The sixth sound causes a rain of amruta (nectar) the divine bliss also

ermed as tears of bliss.

The seventh sound bestows upon the meditator the blessings of being acquainted with the profound and most secret knowledge of Brahman the primordial cosmic energy, the atman as against the mind Uiva).

The eighth sound enables the meditator to speak and understand a mystical language. From here on this is a very sublime stage achieved by very few persons who are on path of spiritual ultimate moksha. He can speak and understand any language and meditate with sublime stage of body.

The ninth sound enables the meditator to make himself invisible and acquire what is described as third eye and also acquires divine power of insight and infinite vision. This is the stage acquired by Rish is and Mahants which common man with no firm resolution can ever achieve.

Finally the tenth sound is the stage of acquiring the transcendental and eclectic knowledge pertaining to the supreme Brahman, the absolute truth. A way to get introduced to sublime presence of Brahman the originator of Vishva, the ever present primordial sound of energy. [These aspects have been described in detail in Nad-Bindu Upanishad of Rig Veda]

The relax actions are controlled by brain. Nerves of the brain are actually an electric circuit consisting of a fine maze of ganglions, nerve fibers and nerve endings much like integrated circuit of computers.

[And these aspects help one to instruct the brain to make subtle changes in what are called strands in DNA of an individual leading to positive changes to nullify the effects of deceases especially of the type of cancer. We will deal with this in detail when we come to that topic in subsequent chapters.]

Through brain these sound waves which are emanating from cosmic sound tend to interfere with and modify their working much like the interference of electronically charged particles of the solar wind with the radio transmission on earth. Similarly the impulses or electric signals which are given by the brain to other parts of the body through meditation also get affected or modified paving the way to change the damaged strands in the DNA in particular manner.

As stated earlier muscles of the body react differently to different frequencies or wavelengths.

तस्मिन्मनो विलीयते मनसि संकल्पविकल्पे दग्धं पुण्यपापे सदाशिव:
शक्यात्मा सर्वत्रावस्थित: स्वयंज्योति: शुद्धो बुद्धो नित्यो निरञ्जन:
शान्तं प्रकाशत इतिवेदानुवचनं भवतीत्युपनिषत् ।।२१।।   हंसोपनिषद

When the mind and the heart dissolve and become one with the indescribable fathomless entity (Brahman the Absolute) and lose their independent identity and existence, then all doubts and confusions, all perplexities and consternations that had existed till this time did not happen, collapse into their primary source, the Mana (emotional as well as thinking mind and the sentimental heart) of the meditator.

Once the duel entity mind and heart cease to exist, there is no scope for one to make so many resolves. Have so many desires. Get involved in so many things pertain to this mundane world. The world itself ceases to exist because the existence of the world is due to mind. It is the mind that conceives and then gives this world a shape as well as importance.

Since the mind and heart do not exist, then all the deeds, whether good or bad cease to matter. Such liberated man is called Hans. He is supposed to be personification of Shiva (truth, bliss, auspiciousness, wisdom, enlightenment). The ultimate goal is therefore to become synonymous with one's Atma exhibiting all virtues of Shiva the all-

pervading and omnipresent, self-enlightened tranquil Brahman.

Before going further to dwell upon spiritual text on methods and importance of meditation let us understand meditation in its real perspective. The words Contemplation and Meditation have to be understood in two perspectives. The dictionary describes 'contemplation as - to reflect and consider, looking at attentively, to study, to intend calmly. This is the meaning of the word in its transitive form. Intransitive verb meaning is to think seriously, attentively. As a noun it means 'a matter of thought. A contemplative mind is one which is inclined to think deeply on any matter. It is the opposite of an impulsive, reckless and restless mind. It is pondering on any subject to weigh the pros and cons of any subject in the mind carefully. But the deep attention and pondering should be discriminative in nature because a person has to have interest in any subject to be able to focus his attention on it for any length of time.

The important fact is that to be positively discriminative is to focus the attention on positive aspects of life rather than degrading negative aspects. While concentrating on positive aspects one must try to delve deeper and deeper in to reality and rise higher and higher in understanding ultimate truth. The word contemplation is derived from the Latin word contemplate which means 'to gaze attentively'. In the mystical and spiritual sense it means 'knowledge consisting in the partial or complete identification of the knower with the object of knowledge with resultant loss of the person's own individuality.' When individualism is lost the person begins to identify himself with the larger perspective of existence in the form of the cosmic nature. This identification of the individual with the cosmos- rather cosmic mind- is synonymous with the identification of his soul with the Supreme Soul or Universal Spirit called Brahma.

The main emphasis of contemplation is on refining and sharpening person's instruments of perception and tuning the mind so that it can perceive the reality behind the facade of variety, a facade which might be illusionary. It is looking inwards in order to grasp the nature of activity going on in the mind-intellect complex.

The word meditation in the context of the mind and intellect means to consider thoughtfully, to revolve in the mind. Contemplation is done in the mind-intellect complex of the person. It requires little or no physical exercise or minimal focused and diligent involvement of the physical body. Contemplation requires steadfastness of mind persistent and consistent efforts and deep attention of the mind without which focusing of it is not

possible. A focus mind acquires the precision and prowess of laser beam; it becomes precise and surgical and becomes penetrating and potent.

Contemplation induces the urge to explore the dimension of silence as well as meditation. It confers a quietness and steadiness in persons behavior with others. It leads to spontaneous self-restraint and puts a leash on the process of verbalization which is characteristic of modern man and exercise which is nothing more than a Waste of one's vital energy.

There are four functions of the mind which are sensing, feeling, thinking and contemplating. By sensing the mind perceives the world around it through the sense organs and its ability to stimulate the organs of action. By feeling the mind experiences the senses of joy and pleasures or sorrows and pains, love and anger. These two functions are the actions of mind. The third function of thinking is then taken over by the intellect. This intellect is the captain of the mind. Whereas the mind is the servant, the intellect is the boss. By thinking the intellect with the help from mind tries to understand and decipher the true nature of the world, the inputs of the sense organs and decides on their proper responses. Thinking relies a lot on the memory bank of the mind-intellect complex to take a decision. Finally by contemplation the intellect take some time off in private and thinks deeply, intently, weighing the pros and cons of any matter which are not part of the routine day to day work of the complex. Thinking therefore leads to contemplation. The intellect tries to unravel the mystery around it and so it thinks and thinks deeper and still deeper in a process we call contemplation. (Here we must take a note that this is a stage in meditation which helps a person in contemplating needed modification in his DNA to try to free himself in the deceases to which he is subjected. We will deal with this in detail in next chapter).

To take an example, a person may learn any chapter by repeating it mentally. But he needs to think while answering question on it. Contemplation inspires him to think beyond the apparent lessons of the chapter to search for those aspects which are not covered in the lesson. This require further investigation, research, pondering, quest and to look ahead. It's deeper than simple thinking.

Meditation in precise is a more physical exercise involving several time tasted practical techniques such as controlling of breath, focusing of the mind on some image, spot or sound. These exercises are part of yoga. A vagrant and agitated mind is forcefully pinned down on an object so as to

calm it down. The mind in this state is conscious and aware of the agitations and is directing the body to calm down. The intellect is guiding the mind to calm down its agitations.

Meditative practices can alter a Person's health, mental state, emotions, and individual identity and provide him with calmness of his behavior with others, a sense of well-being and a purpose of life. Aim of the meditation is self-identification and self-realization. For without self-purification, self-realization is not possible.

So far we have studied the meditation, its definition and its practical and theosophical meaning. Now let us see what Upanishads and spiritual texts advise us on this all important topic.

The purpose of meditation or dhyana is to become consciously aware of or investigate into one's own mind and body to know oneself. It is essentially an exclusive as well as an inclusive process, in which one withdraws one's mind and senses from the distractions of the world and contemplates upon a chosen object or idea with concentration. It is focused thinking with or without the exercise of individual will, in which the mind and the body has to be brought together to function as one harmonious whole. With the help of meditation we can overcome our mental blocks, negative thinking, debilitating fears, stress and anxiety by knowing their cause and dealing with them. In dhyana we gain insightful awareness whereby we can control over our responses and reactions. Through its regular practice, we come to understand the nature of things, the impermanence of our corporeal existence, the fluctuations of our minds, the source of our own suffering and its possible resolution. The difference between meditation and contemplation is mostly academic. According to, some meditation is an insightful observation and contemplation a concentrated reflection, with detachment being the common factor between the two. Both these words are used interchangeably to convey the same meaning as dhayna.

Dhyana is a Sanskrit word. Dhi means receptacle or the mind and yana means moving or going. Dhyana means journey or movement of the mind. It is a mental activity of the mind (dhi). In Hindu philosophy, the mind (manas) is viewed as a receptacle (dhi) into which thoughts pour back and forth from the universal pool of thought forms. According to Hindu tradition, the human mind has the creative potency of God. You become what you think. You are a sum total of your thoughts and desires, not only of this life but also of your past lives. What you think and desire grows upon you,

becomes part of your latent impressions (samskaras) and influence the course of your life here and here after. These samskaras determine the future course of your lives as they accompany you to the next world. All your mental actions are part of your karma as much as any physical action. Even the animals have the ability to evolve into higher being through their mental focus.

Meditation is observing the inward and outward movement of thoughts that are coming and going out of the mind, with silence (maunam), stability (dhiram) and detachment (vairagyam). According to Hindu theories of creation, all the beings and worlds emanated from God (mentioned as Brahma in some scriptures and Brahman in others) through meditation only. Its mysteries and its dimensions can be comprehended in transcendental states of self-absorption which is possible through meditation only. Since each individual is a carbon copy of the universe, by understanding ourselves we can understand the manifest universe. Thus our ancient rishis practiced meditation and contemplation to discover the truths concerning themselves and the world around them. In their deep meditative states they envisioned the Vedic wisdom and Universal Self. Since the knowledge poured forth into their receptive and stabilized minds from the universal consciousness, on its own, without any egoistic intention or selfishness on their part, it is considered as not man made (apaurusheya), but divine and truthful (pramana).

All thoughts and knowledge exist in the universe. We do not create thoughts, although we erroneously believe so, just as we are not the real doers of our actions, as declared in the Bhagavad-Gita, but mere instruments in the hands of God. We can only receive them and make meaning out of them according to the flow of our inclinations, intentions, intellect and attitudes. The most exalted spiritual truths are revealed to us in our moments of reverential silence, when our minds are focused, the senses and the self-sense are asleep and the desires are extinguished. The six Hindu schools of philosophy are so called darshanas (visions) because they are products of such receptive process in which knowledge was envisioned (darshanam) in the pit of the human mind that was untainted by the impurities of worldly life. While the followers of respective schools may argue or quarrel about the merits and demerits of their respective systems of philosophy, from a spiritual perspective, we hold them to be different standpoints of the same universal knowledge revealed to man at different points of time in history, and like any other standpoint they represent a particular view of the reality and do not wholly represent the universal reality itself, which is well rounded, eternal, infinite and absolute in itself without divisions, grades and contradictions.

The Vedic seers did not use the word dhyana in the early Vedic theology. But through their own personal experience, they were aware of the importance of the mind and its ability to manifest things. They viewed creation as the mental manifestation of the Isvara or Brahman, the universal Self and they believe through austerities and penances man could acquire similar potencies. The creation of an alternate heaven (trishanku) by sage Viswamitra is a case in point. According to Jennie Miller, a British scholar, the Vedic prayer was a form of dhyana in which the two sense functions, "vision and sound, seer ship and singing are intimately connected."

The Vedic concept of dhayna or meditation seems to have evolved gradually with the emergence of Upanishadic thought and the idea that man personified the entire universe within himself and by himself and that hidden deep within him was an eternal principle that was Universal Self in its individual aspect. Either man (purusha) was a projection of the universe in its own mode or the universe was a projection of the individual self (purusha) in its own form. Both views enjoyed patronage of scholarly minds. If the former was true, our existence was ephemeral and part of a much larger dream, and if the latter was true, then the universe might be an illusion. In either proposition the world is seen as unreal or illusory, a view that caught the attention of Hindu scholars for centuries and found its way into the monistic (advaita) philosophy of Shankaracharya.

Miller proposed the view that in the beginning the Vedic seers held Brahman to be a meditative state, not a universal entity. She suggested that the Vedic seers practiced three different types of meditation and were familiar with three states of transcendental reality, which they identified with Brahman. In addition they were also familiar with the forth state although it was not explicitly mentioned in the early Vedic hymns. They are:

♦   Mantric meditation or meditation on the Vedic mantras with concentration,

♦   Visual meditation or meditation on a particular deity with illumined thought,

♦   Absorption in mind and heart or meditation on illumined insight residing in the mind and the heart.

Samadhi or the experience of the ecstatic state of Brahman was the fourth state of Brahman, which is not mentioned in the Rigveda but described in the Mandukya Upanishad as the Fourth state (turiya).

The early Vedic hymns may not mention the word dhyana or dharana explicitly, but we have indications in the scriptures to believe that the Rigvedic seers were familiar with contemplative and meditative methods of self-enquiry. The Upanishads are not speculative works of human imagination, but revelatory scriptures envisioned by the Seers as they were exploring the riddles of human existence. Similarly the Vedic hymns, constituting the samhitas, were transmitted to them in deep meditative states.

Descriptions of meditation practice in the Upanishads

In the Upanishads words such as dhaya, dhvai, manta, drushti, and mati are used to denote meditation. Tapas was a more popular spiritual practice in which meditation formed part of a set of austerities and penances that were aimed to generate bodily heat or inner fire to burn away the impurities of the mind and the body. Tapas were rooted in Vedic tradition, a system by itself, having its own body of practices, which thrived prior to the emergence of the classical yoga as a standard spiritual practice. It was practiced by many seers and sages of the Vedic and epic age, who believed that tapas was the source of the creative potency even in case of gods. According to the Rigveda, the word emanated from the primordial Being by the great heat of austerity (tapas). Another word that is used in the Upanishads frequently to denote meditation is 'upasana', a meditative practice that seems to have gradually evolved into dhyana. Compared to upasana, dhyana is a more concentrated and meditative practice without the outward ritual component and the devotional fervor.

The word upasana is used in the Upanishads in a boarder sense to denote ritual worship or service, with or without the employment of udgita (Aum), ritual chants or sacrificial mantras. The practice seems to have developed with the evolution of the Vedic thought, as is evident in the Briahdaranyaka Upanishad, one of the earliest Upanishads, which led to the identification of the human body with the cosmos (see brihadarnyakopanishad chapter1 and 2), internalization of Vedic ritual and internal worship, through contemplation, of various divinities such as the vital breaths, fire, water, speech, mind, the eyes, the body and the consciousness, each representing a particular aspect of the manifest

creation. In this progressive form of meditation, which proceeded from the outer to the inner, worshipping the inmost Self or Brahman was considered to be the best. (Brihadaranyakopnishad chapter 2, first Brahmana.)

These early ideas gradually gave way to more advanced forms of meditation which sought to control the mind and the body for experiencing various transcendental states of consciousness. The knowledge of these states was kept confidential and expressed mostly in symbolic terms. Brahman was now recognized as the highest and supreme Reality rather than mere meditative state. The realization that beyond all divinities existed the resplendent and innermost Self and that it could be attained.

The Chandogya Upanishad

The Chandogya Upanishad reflects this progressive development in the Vedic thought. The Upanishad views meditation or contemplation (dhyna) as a journey into oneself till one reaches the reality that is permanent, reliable and beyond which there is nothing else to be found or realized. It explains the various ways in which one can meditate upon Aum (udgita). In a conversation between Narada and Sanatkumara, which is recorded in the Upanishad, the latter explains the progressive forms of meditation (upasana) upon the various aspects of the mind and the body, from the outer to the inner, in order to overcome suffering and realize the true nature of Brahman. He begins by saying that one should meditate (upasana) upon the name (nama) as Brahman, then the speech (vak), then the mind (manas), then the chitt consciousness (chitta), then contemplation (dhyana), then intelligence (vidnyanam), then strength (balam), then food (Annam), then water, then heat, then ether and so on. Each of these methods of meditations said to result in some specific benefit.

The Katha Upanishad

The Katha Upanishad also suggests a similar approach by emphasizing the need to stabilize the mind through the practice of self-contemplation (adhyatma yoga) to overcome both joy and sorrow and realize Brahman who is difficult to be seen (durdasam), deeply hidden (gudham), inside a cave (guhatitam) and dwells in the deep (gahvarestham).

Realizing through self-contemplation that primal God, difficult to be seen, deeply hidden, set in the cave (of the heart), dwelling in the deep, the wise man leaves behind both joy and sorrow.

The Svetasvatara Upanishad

The Svetasvatara Upanishad, with its definitive leanings towards Shaivism, mentions the word "dhyana-yoga" and "dhyana" which suggests the changing times and the systematization of the knowledge of yoga. It declares that those who practiced dhayna-yoga saw the self-power of the divine (devatma shakti) hidden in His own qualities (sva gunair nigudham) as the first cause (karanam) of creation, which they understood in their contemplative mode as a rotating wheel having fifty spokes (energies), three tires (qualities) and one hub (Isvara or God). In creation there is perishable matter (pradhana) and imperishable Lord (Hara). By meditating upon Him, uniting with him and reflecting upon Him one is freed from illusion of the world (maya nivrutti).

The Upanishad also explains how meditation should be performed. It is by using the body as the lower friction stick (arani) and the syllable Aum (pranava) as the upper friction stick one may see hidden God (devam) in meditation. This effort has to be accompanied by truthfulness (satyam) and austerity (tapas). According to the Upanishad, yoga of which dhyana is an important component, is a cleansing process. Just as a mirror covered with dust is able to reflect well when it is cleaned, when through yoga we overcome the illusion and ignorance we have about ourselves and our existence, we are able to discern the Universal Self hidden in all as the source of all and transcend death.

Maitri Upanishad

According to Maitri Upanishad, Prajapati Brahma, the creator god, being alone and unhappy, meditated upon himself (atmanam abhdhyat) and differentiated himself into diverse beings. When he found them to be lifeless and inert like stone, he entered into them and divided himself into five breaths and the internal fire (vaisvanara). Then, residing in the heart, he pierced five openings in each body and through them began enjoying things using the five senses as his reigns. The Upanishad further states that when the soul resides in the body and mind which is made up of the elements, it is known as the elemental-self (bhutatma). The elemental-self does not remember its highest state (parama padam) because of ignorance. It becomes free from such an evil existence (papam) only when it gains the knowledge of Brahman (Brahma vidya) through the triad, namely knowledge (vidya), austerity (tapas) and meditation (chintana). The Upanishad distinguishes two types of Brahman, the one with form and

the other without form. Of the two, the formless Brahman is real, upon whom one should meditate as Aum to become united with Him.

The Six fold Yoga

Apart from the three fold practice mentioned above, the Maitri Upanishad has prescribed six fold yoga (sadhanga yoga) for the liberation of the elemental soul from both good and evil. It consists of control of breath (pranayama), withdrawal of the senses (pratyahara), meditation (dhyanam), dharana (concentration), logical enquiry (tarka) and self-absorption (Samadhi). In contrast to the classical yoga of Patanjali, in this yoga, concentration (dharana) comes after dhyana. Probably in this system dhyana means passive meditation and tarka means concentrated meditation. According to S.Radhakrishnan, it is contemplative enquiry or reflective self-absorption (savitarka Samadhi). "It may also mean an enquiry whether the mind has become transformed or not into object of meditation or investigation into the hindrances of concentration caused by the inferior powers acquired by meditation." Swhetashvara Upanishad. The Upanishad mentions a higher concentration technique of seeing Brahman through contemplative thought (tarka), known as lumbika-yoga. It consists of holding the tip of the tongue down the palate, restraining the speech, the mind and the breath and seeing the (shining) self through the (elemental or impure) self.

The Paingala Upanishad

The Paingala Upanishad distinguishes four kinds of spiritual practice to attain Brahman and explains the purport of each. They are hearing (shravanam), reflection (mananam), meditation (nidhidhaysanam) and self-realization (atma darshana). Investigation into the meaning and purpose (vakyartha vichara) of the Vedic mantras such as "Thou art That," and "I am Brahman," constitute hearing (shravanam). Paying undivided attention to what is being heard is reflection. Concentrating the thought solely on what has been understood through hearing and reflection is meditation. When the distinction between the subject and the object disappears in the heightened state of concentration, it is called cognition of the self (atma darshana). With it all the karmas become destroyed and one experiences a shower of supreme bliss coming from thousand directions. The wise call such a state as dharma megha samadhi (self-absorption of the virtuous kind). As all the impurities are removed and the past and present karmas are neutralized, the knower of Brahman becomes a

liberated being Uivan mukta). When the time of his departure from this world comes, he leaves his embodied state and enters into the supreme state of non-movement (aspandatam), which is eternal, devoid of sensations, constant, alone and perfect.

The Kaivalya Upanishad

The Kaivalya Upanishad emphasizes the importance of devotion in the practice of yoga and meditation. It idcntifies faith (shraddha), devotion (bhakti), meditation (dhyana) and concentration as the means to know Brahman who is equated with Shiva. One should meditate upon the lotus of the heart which is pure, without passion, where in lies the source of Brahma who is eternal. Blue throated and companion of Uma.

The Bhagavad-Gita

In the Bhagavad-Gita, Lord Krishna touches upon the subject of dhyana on many occasions during the course of his long conversation with Arjuna. Verses 1 Oto 16 in the 6th chapter entitled, Dhyana Yoga, explain how and in what conditions a yogi should subdue his mind through concentration. Living alone in solitude, in a clean place covered with kusa grass, a deer skin and a cloth, one over the other, on a firm seat, a yogi, who is pure and self-controlled, without desires and free from possessions, should sit with his body, head and neck erect and concentrate his mind upon the tip of the nose. With concentration and subdued mind, he eventually attains lasting peace. So although the chapter is entitled the yoga of meditation (dhyana yoga), it basically speaks about the practice of concentration to control the mind and the senses. The same chapter defines yoga as disconnection from union with pain. In Chapter 12 meditation is described to be superior to knowledge and renunciation of the fruit of action better than meditation from which peace follows immediately. In Chapter 13 it is said that through dhyana one can see the Self in the Self by the Self.

Dhyana in Yogasutra

Dhyana is an important limb of the eightfold (Ashtanga) yoga of Patanajali, whose work the Yogasutra, considered as the most authoritative ancient treatise on

Yoga, presents the practice of Yoga in a systematic and orderly manner. The eight limbs of yoga are inter related and are not meant to be practiced in isolation. The purpose of yoga is to control the fluctuations of the chitta and facilitate its stability by cultivating

purity (sattva) through a cleansing process so that one can become absorbed in oneself and realize his true identity. Of the eightfold yoga, meditation (dhyana) is penultimate limb, preceded by yama, niyama, pranayama, pratyahara, asana, dharana and followed by samadhi. All the limbs are important and complimentary. In other words success in meditation depends upon the progress achieved in other areas, especially the ones preceding it in the order. So is the case with Samadhi, which is not possible unless there is perfection in all the other areas of yoga. Dhyana is an important component of classical yoga. According to Patanjali stability of the mind can be achieved by practicing meditation of objects that are pleasing to us (Yatabhimata dhyanat va). In the third section of the Yogasutra he defines dhyana as the steady (pratyata) and continuous flow of awareness (ekantata) towards the same point.

The Puranas and the symbolism

The epics and the Puranas are replete with the stories of seers, sages and gods practicing yoga, tapas and other forms of spiritual practices. Some of the stories have deep symbolism, such as the story of the churning of the oceans (sagara manthanam) in which gods and demons come together to churn the ocean to extract the elixir (amrita). The story symbolically represents various yogic practices which culminate in immortality. In the story the ocean represents the chitta (often referred as the mind stuff or chitt consciousness) which is subject to mental fluctuations (chitta vruttis). The gods and demons represent the pure and impure thoughts and energies of the mind and the body (the physical realm). The serpent Vasuki represents desire or the Vaishvanara fire. The mount mandhara represents concentration (dharana) of the mind (manas). The churning represents the reflective or contemplative process in search of immortality. The poison that emerged during the churning represents the pain and suffering generated from the practice of austerities (tapas). Lord Shiva represents the teacher who takes upon himself the suffering of his sincere disciples. The various magical objects that came out of the ocean during the churning represent the various perfections (siddhis) or supernatural powers described in the Yogasutra. Dharana (concentration) is focused bare attention and dhyana is focused meditation.

Dhyana and tantra

Shaivism has many sects and each has its own set of techniques and theories of yoga, rooted in the theoretical and philosophical aspects of Shaiva religious texts (Agama) and tantras some of which are left handed (Vamachara) and some right handed (Sadacara). The former use the mind and body, intoxicants, sexual intercourse and socially reprehensible behavior as a part of their self-cleansing process to achieve self-realization. All sects of Shaivism and Shaktism worship Shiva or Shakti or both and aim to achieve union with them through various practices of which meditation or dhyana is an important component. Symbols and images of Shiva and Shakti and various mystic diagrams (Yantras) used religious worship, meditation and concentration, apart from proper conduct and devotion to keep the mind pure and elevated. The yoga traditions of Shaivims go by different names such as hatha yoga, tantra yoga and Kundalini yoga. According to Kularnava Tantra, one of the well-known texts of Kaula tradition composed during the medieval period, meditation is of two type coarse (sthula) and subtle (sukshma). The former is meditation on form, usually an object, image or symbol and the latter meditation on the formless, usually an abstract concept or state of Shiva as pure and resplendent light, bliss. In both types of meditation, the mind has to become stable or immobile and the distinction between the subject and object should disappear to achieve the ecstatic state of self-absorption (Samadhi).

Meditation in hatha yoga

Hatha yoga is an important offshoot of Tantrism, which aims to develop the human body, through various ascetic and yogic practices, into a strong diamond (vajra) like and divine body that would be strong and pure enough to house the splendor of Shiva or Shakti. When the body is transmuted and filled with light and the higher spiritual energies it becomes a fit vehicle for enlightenment and possession extraordinary powers and abilities (siddhis) such as the will to assume any form and live in the subtle regions in the subtle body at will. Hatha yoga is followed by many traditions of Shaivism but it was made popular by the Natha tradition established by Gorakshanath who probably lived between 10th and 11th century C.E. Hatha yoga has many features common with the classical yoga but differ from the latter with regard to the intensity and intent of such practices. Hatha yoga used more painful and austere physical posture and cleansing processes to perfect the mind and body and make it fit for transcendental experiences. Gheranda Samhita prescribes six acts of purification for this

purpose of which meditation (dhyana) is one. According to it, the postures (asana) make the body strong, the gestures (mudras) make it stable, sense withdrawal (pratyahara) leads to calmmess, breath control (pranayama) brings lightness, dhyana leads to the perception of the self and with Samadhi comes the ecstatic union. Dhauli, basti, neti, lauli, trataka and kapala-bhati are the important and more specific techniques suggested by the scripture for cleansing the various part of the mind and the body. It also mentions three types of dhyana:

♦ Visualization of coarse objects (sthula dhyana), considered to be the least effective of all

♦ Contemplation of Absolute being as the light (tejo dhyana) which is said to be a hundred times better than the above.

♦ Visualization of subtle objects (sukshma dhayna) such as the

essence of the Self, which is said to be the greatest of all and hundred times better than the meditation on light.

The Goraksha Paddathi describes meditation as two fold, "composite (sakala) and impetrate (nishkala). It is composite because of differences in performance. And impetrate also because of differences in performance," which is also devoid of qualities (nirguna). Meditation has to be practiced by visualizing the various chakras in detail concentrating with focus on the serpent (kunadlini) starting from the base (muladhara) and gradually moving upward to the top of the head (adnya-chakra). "Anus, penis, navel, lotus, the one above that (i.e., the throat), the bell, the place of 'hanger' (i.e. The Uvula), the spot between the eyebrows, and the space cavity (at the crown of the head)," are the nine locations (sthanas) of the body for focusing the mind and practicing visual meditation. It is important to remember that these techniques should not be followed in isolation but in conjunction with the remaining five acts of purification described above.

Jain yoga

Our knowledge of Jain yoga comes to us mainly from the work of writers like Haribhadra Suri (8th century C.E). Jain yoga shares some common features with the yoga traditions of Hinduism and probably derived some of the concepts and practices from the classical yoga of Patanjali. Have two components:

a preparatory course (purva seva) meant for the lay followers who

have become disillusioned with their worldly lives and embarked upon a journey of liberation (apunar bandhaka)

And the yoga proper meant for the more advanced practitioners,

who have advanced on the path and have achieved some degree of right or mixed vision (samyag drushti).

Yoga for the lay followers consists of ritual worship (pujana), proper conduct (sadachara), austerities (tapas), and no negative feelings towards liberation (mukti advesha). Five levels of practice are suggested for the advanced followers: centering in the self (adhyatma yoga), contemplation (bhavana), meditation (dhyana), equanimity (samata), cessation of the modifications (vrutti samskhaya) of the consciousness. Dhayna or meditation is to be practiced everyday one or more times, but at least once for 48 minutes, by all followers of Jainism as per the techniques prescribed in their tradition.

Dhyana in Buddhism

The purpose of yoga in Buddhism is to cultivate right attentiveness of the mind and the body and control the movements of the mind so that one can experience peace and equanimity (Samantha). Buddhism does not believe in the existence of soul. So unlike in classical yoga or in Hinduism, annihilation of the ego-sense or the ephemeral and aggregate personality rather than realization of the self is the ultimate goal of Buddhist yoga. Through meditation practitioners of Buddhism aim to develop insight into themselves, how they think and act motivated by various desires and subjects themselves to suffering in numerous ways. Thus, understanding and awareness or insight and mindfulness are the two important elements of Buddhist dhyana. Balance or the middle approach is another important aspect of this practice so that we will neither over indulge nor neglect our duty to meditate regularly. As regards to the postures (asanas), breath control (pranayama) withdrawal of the senses (pratyahara), methods and meditation and states of self-absorption, there is a correlating between the yogic practices of Buddhism and Hinduism. But as we have already said, the difference lies mainly in the intent and the ultimate purpose of all of the practices.

In truth, in Buddhism, every aspect of the mundane life, every activity and movement of the mind and the body can be an object of meditation. Various techniques are followed to cultivate insightful awareness and end suffering, such as tranquility (Samantha) meditation, insightful (vipassana) meditation In Samantha meditation a meditator sits in a quietly place, closing his eyes and calmly and rather passively lets go of

his thoughts and desires with detachment, with his attention focused on his breathing. Whenever his attention is strayed, he brings it back to his breath. Regular practice of this meditation said to result in calmness of the mind (Samantha). Insight meditation, also known as vipassana meditation, involves a deep exploration of all the movements that arise in the consciousness with mindfulness and detachment. When a mediator becomes mindful of the contents of his mind, he develops a deep understanding of the source of his suffering and the impermanence of the world and eventually experiences peace. Sitting meditation and walking meditation are other popular forms of meditation in Buddhism. Dhyana is not meant to be practiced in isolation but as a part of various other practices which are meant to prepare the mind and the body to experience altered states of consciousness and assimilate higher forms of energy without side effects.

In Western medicinal practice experiments has recently discovered the powerful effects of meditation, by allowing doctors to treat the body and the mind. In reality, the mind is a very misunderstood and unexplored region of the human existence. Modern science knows more about the composition of the earth than it does about the mechanics of the human brain. Yet, meditation thwarts all notions of modern medicine with its shocking ability to take obscure visualizations and create physical responses in the body. Mahayana Buddhism, found mainly in the autonomous region of Tibet, has become the main reference and standard for meditation practices in the west. Tibetans have used meditation for centuries as treatment for illness, and now, modern medicine of the western world is just beginning to reap the benefits of this unique and unconventional treatment for a variety of physical and mental ailments. Once a practice reserved strictly for Buddhist monks, meditation has become a worldwide phenomenon. In our next Chapter on meditation and DNA we will explore in more detail the relevance of meditation in effecting changes in DNA for getting some help in reducing the ill effects or relief from certain deceases.

GENETIC CODE

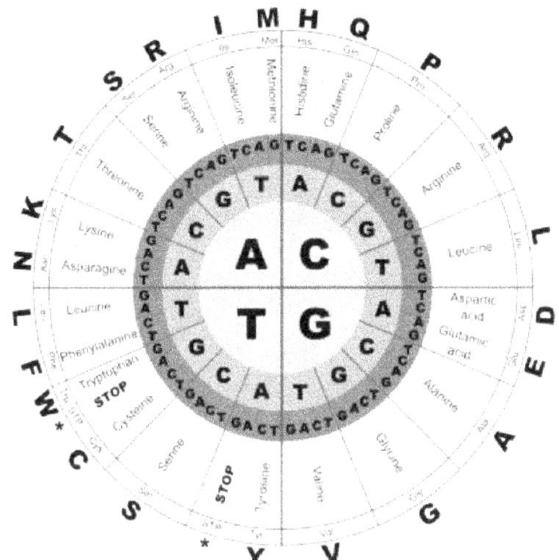

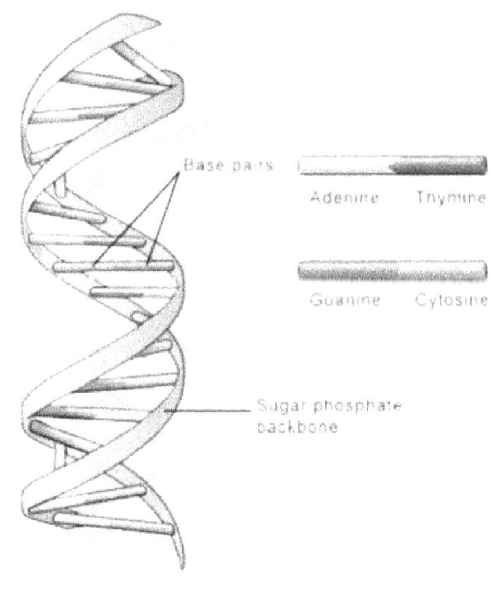

Dia.2

- Replication of DNA
  - base pairing
  - new strand is 1/2 parent template &
    1/2 new DNA
    - semi-conservative copy process

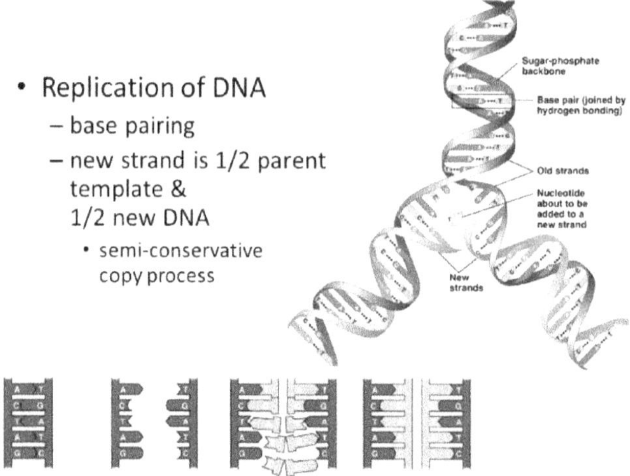

Dia.3

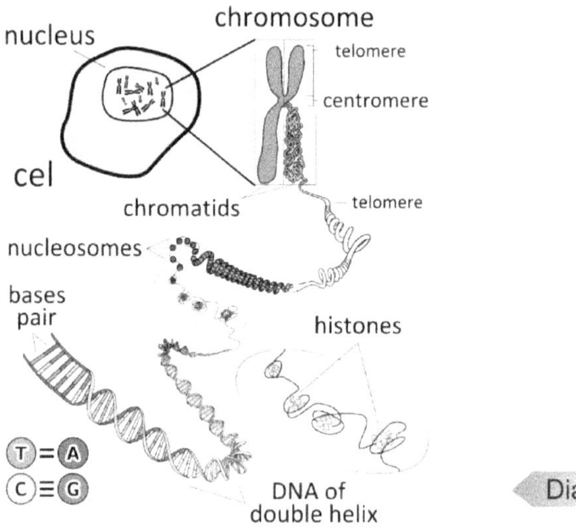

Dia.4

MEDITATION AND DNA

Before going to discussion of how Mediation can be a tool to effect changes in DNA let us see what meant by DNA.

What is DNA?

DNA, or deoxyribonucleic acid, is the hereditary material in humans and almost all other organisms. Nearly every cell in a person's body has the same DNA. Most DNA is located in the cell nucleus (where it is called nuclear DNA), but a small amount of DNA can also be found in the mitochondria (where it is called mitochondrial DNA or mt DNA).

The information in DNA is stored as a code made up of four chemical bases:

1.Adenine (A) 2.Guanine (G) 3.Cytosine (C) and 4.Thymine (T).

Human DNA consists of about 3 billion bases, and more than 99 percent of those bases are the same in all people. The order, or sequence, of these bases determines the information available for building and maintaining an organism, similar to the way in which letters of the alphabet appear in a certain order to form words and sentences.

DNA bases pair up with each other, A with T and C with G, to form units called base pairs. Each base is also attached to a sugar molecule and a phosphate molecule. Together, a base, sugar, and phosphate are called a nucleotide. Nucleotides are arranged in two long strands that form a spiral called a double helix. The structure of the double helix is somewhat like a ladder, with the base pairs forming the ladder's rungs and the sugar and phosphate molecules forming the vertical sidepieces of the ladder. (See figure below)

An important property of DNA is that it can replicate, or make copies of itself. Each strand of DNA in the double helix can serve as a pattern for duplicating the sequence of bases. This is critical when cells divide because each new cell needs to have an exact copy of the DNA present in the old cell. DNA is a double helix formed by base pairs attached to a sugar-phosphate backbone.

See the diagram Dia.2

Now let us take into consideration another expiation for changes in structure of DNA while copying out the new life. Research indicates that hypothesis of a hidden intelligence contained within the DNA of all living things is interesting. What is this intelligence? Intelligence comes from the Latin inter-legere, to choose between. There seems to be a capacity to make choices operating inside each cell in our body, down to the level of individual proteins and enzymes. DNA itself is a kind of text that functions through a coding system called genetic code, which is strikingly similar to codes used by human beings.

Some enzymes edit the RNA transcript of the DNA text and add new letters to it; any error made during this editing can be fatal to the entire organism; so these enzymes are consistently making the right choices; if they don't, something often goes wrong leading to cancer and other diseases.

Cells send one another signals, in the form of proteins and molecules. These signals mean: divide, or don't divide, move, or don't move, kill yourself, or stay alive. Any one cell is listening to hundreds of signals at the same time, and has to integrate them and decide what to do. DNA is a

single molecule with a double helix structure; it is two complementary versions of the same "text" wrapped around each other; this allows it to unwind and make copies of itself: twins! This twinning mechanism is at the heart of life since it began. Without it, one cell could not become two, and life would not exist. And, from one generation to the next, the DNA text can also be modified, so it allows both consistancy and transformation. This means that beings can be the same and not the same. One of the mysteries is what drives the changes in the DNA text in evolution. DNA has apparently been around for billions of years in its current form in virtually all forms of life.

The old theory - random accumulation of errors combined with natural selection - does not fully explain the data currently generated by genome sequencing. The question is wide open. The structure of DNA as we know it is made up of letters and thus has a specific text and language. You could say our bodies are made up of language, yet we assume that speech arises from the mind. How do we access this hidden language? Dia.3

The figure Dia.4 explans how chromosomes act in DNA nucleodes.

Once you accept the situation scientifically that the DNA Code is code language of a living beings life and main theme on which the life is in existence and without it there's no life we come to vedantic principle that this world is the manifestation of primordial sound OM continuously vibrating and through it immerged different letters and phonics which is the basis of any life form. Taking into consideration this structural explanations that science offers about DNA we are analyzing and explore our desire of the Absolute (Brahmand) for giving self-expressions as many and how it permeates through its manifestations, non-sentient and sentient, in virtually the same manner in various stages of progress. Nadabindupanishad describes this manifestation in a very profound manner.

ॐ अकारो दक्षिण: पक्ष उकारस्तुत्तर: स्मृत: ।
मकारं पुच्छमित्याहुरर्धमात्रा तु मस्तकम् ॥१॥

Om akaro daxjnah paksha ukarastuttarah smrutah/ makaram puchchamityahurdhamatra tu mastakam /11 ॥

NItyanupashad

The divine cosmic Sound OM has been visualized as a swan. The syllable A of the word OM is compared to right wing of the Swan. The syllable or the vowel U is compared with the left wing, and the syllable M is designated its tail. The half syllable (ardha matra) is the head.

Here we must note that the swan is considered as a very pure and respected bird. It is synonymous with erudition, knowledge and wisdom as well as the ability to pick and choose what is good and living behind what is bad. It is therefore the mound over which the Goddess of speech, knowledge, wisdom and education (Saraswati) sits. The Swan is also reputed to peak pearls from amongst a collection of other jewels and from whatever is offered to it. Also it drinks milk leaving water behind. Here we must take into account from modern science that through the peculiar reaction or catalyst action the four principle chemicals called T G C P described above either pick the necessary language code for remaking duplicate life form or choose the new DNA code to form new life form. The idea that brahmand is created through manifestation of different forms of primordial Sound that is Nad is well recognized by the Vedanta philosophy. Only the language is different suitable to then available sources.

पादादिकं गुणास्तस्य शरीरं तत्वमुच्यते ।
धर्मोऽस्य दक्षिणं चक्षुरधर्मोऽथो परः स्मृत्तः ॥१२॥

Padadikam gunastasya shatiram tattvamuchyate / dharmosya daxinam chxurdharmotho patah smrutah/12/1

Nadbindupanishad

This Swan symbolizes OM has two legs representing the two qualities called 'Raja' and 'Tama'. While its body is the first quality called 'Sat'. 'Dharma' is the right eye while the opposite of 'Dharma' that is Adahrma is the left eye. Here again the Upanishad tries to tell you that in formation of new life selecting the pattern is a must thing. Here the three qualities you must remember are 'Sat 'which is the noblest and most virtuous quality in a creature. 'Raja 'is medium quality of worldly desires and passions. 'Tama' is the meanest quality which leads to evil, vices, inertia etc. 'Dharma' is generally defined as the qualities of righteousness, noble and virtuous

conducts and thought. Since, as we have seen above, the form of life depends upon the language code which defines its structure, the forms of life which emerge is combination of creature's desire or attitude depending upon it's prarabdha in previous lives.

भूर्लोक: पादयोस्तस्य भुवर्लोकस्तु जानुनी ।
सुवर्लोक: कटिदेशे नाभिदेशे महर्जगत ।।३।।

Bhurlokah padayostasya bhuavrlokstu januni / suvarlokah katideshe nabhideshe maharjagatl/3//

Nadbindupanishad

Swan's two legs represent the earth called 'bhuva' it's head represents the celestial world 'Bhuvah'. Its waist area symbolizes the heavens called 'Svah'and it's navel is designated as Maharloka.

Here you must notice that slowly the Upanishad is decoding the life formation from language codes available. In Vedanta literature 14 mythical abodes are described (from Padma Purana).

They are (A) the upper worlds called 'Urdhwa Lokas' which are seven: (i) Bhuva (ii) Bhuvah, (iii)Svah, (iv) Mahah, (v) Janah, (vi) Tapah and (vii) Satyam. (B) The seven nether worlds are called Adhah Loka. They are (i) Atala, (ii) Vitala, (iii) Sutala,(iv) Rasatala, (v) Talatala, (vi) Mahatala and

(vii) Patala.

Thus there are 14 mythical worlds or Abodes. Upanishads do discus the traveling of individual sublime particle termed individual Atman through these worlds but that is a different topic not relevant here.

जनोलोकस्तु हृद्देशे कण्ठे लोकस्तपस्ततः।
भ्रुवोर्ललाटमध्ये तु सत्यलोको व्यवस्थितः ।।४।।

Janolokatu hruddeshe kanthe /okastpsttah / bhruvorlalatmadhye tu satya loko vyavasthitah /14/1

Nadabinupanishad

The Janaloka is present in its heart and Tapa Loka is present in its throat. Satya Loka is present between its eye brows and forehead.

Summary of shlokas 5-14 of this Nadbindupanishad enlighten us about the reality of this world and its spiritual structure which seeker of moksha has to realize through meditation on Nada brahma. The divine Swan described above represents the cosmic attributes of the word OM as well as cosmic gross manifestation in the form of various worlds. The wise erudite who is seeking moksha continuously involves in worshiping NAO brahma 'Pranava' (OM). The patron deity of OM is fire; its form is also like fire. The second syllable U is called 'Vayavya'. The patron deity of it is 'Vayu' (Wind) and its contours, shape; color etc. is charestically like wind. OM is as potent and stupendous as the fire and the wind.

The third syllable M is like the Sun. The 4th syllable is Chandra bindu

(⬤). Has 'Varuna' (water) as its patron deity. This means OM also has

powers of the Sun and Water. Each of the four Matras discussed above has three phases or dimensions or magnitudes (ofilt151£1sfq) each. Therefore, the total number of phases or magnitudes called 'Kalas' of the entire living world's spectrum comes to twelve. One can realize them and recognize through deep meditation, concentration and focus.

Now out of these twelve 'Kalas' (matras) the First is 'Ghoshini'

Second is called 'Vidyunmatra'

Third is 'Patangini'

Fourth is 'Vayuvegini'

Fifth kala (matra) is called 'Namadheya' Sixth is termed as'Aindri'

Seventh is 'Vaishnavi'

Eighth is called 'Shankari'

Ninth matra is called 'Mahati

Tenth is 'Dhruti'

Eleventh is 'Nari'

Twelveth is called 'Brahmi'.

We must note here that the harmonization between the vibrations emanating from the heart as well as electromagnetic waves from the brain of a person create different language codes to form innumerable newliving forms. We know that OM consists of different sound waves giving rise to sounds which denotes particular Alphabet or vowel. The individual Atman which is part and parcel of primordial cosmic Sound recognized as OM then culminates into new life.

We had seen already in our discussion relating to DNA formation that letters T G PC which denotes specific chemicals react chemically through brain and minds'. This reaction culminates into a peculiar DNA formation. In the process of selecting chromosomes DNA nucleoside pick up a code language from a genetic code (See Dia.1) which forms duplication of existing life or by process of elimination by default new double helix to give rise to new species. Here before proceeding further with our discussion on Nadbindupanishad let us consider one important aspect of Vedanta theory about utilization of genetic language code that is karmic previous life in the formation or negation of existing form or its modification or total rejection allowing it to integrate into sublime Brahman; the ultimate goal of a person in spiritual rearm.

In the discussion above we have already noted that both modern science and Vedanta agree that astral mass of the world is nothing but the code languages of the genetic code in different forms forming plethora of innumerable forms. Therefore it is well established that Sound is a very powerful mind-expanding tool. In various spiritual traditions all around the world, people utilize the power of sound through the form of mantras. A mantra is a syllable, word, or group of words used to bring about changes in consciousness by the agency of sounds and vibrations. The word mantra consists of the Sanskrit root man or "to think" and the suffix tra, referring to tools or instruments. Thus, its literal meaning would be "instrument of thought."

A mantra's effect, however, does not merely come from its corresponding conceptual meaning, but instead from its inherent potential to produce a specific mental or physical result. If you understand the relationship between vibration and consciousness, you will understand how mantras work. Vibration and consciousness are so intimately connected that there is a specific relationship existing between each kind of vibration and the particular aspect of consciousness gives expression to

it. In other words, wherever there is a manifestation of consciousness, there is vibration associated with it whether we are able to trace it or not.

To better understand this relationship, let's take a look at how it is expressed at the lowest level of manifestation, i.e., in sensory perception. For example, each particular vibration of light with a definite wavelength produces its corresponding color, which we then perceive with our eyes. In music, each particular vibration of sound becomes evident in our consciousness through the form of musical notes, which we can then hear through our ears. In principle, certain kinds of vibration can be matched with corresponding states or levels of consciousness. This simply means that if you want to reach a specific state of consciousness, you can do so by initiating a particular kind of vibration by chanting a mantra. Remember that vibrations can influence matter and cause changes in matter as well, so aside from affecting us psychologically, mantras may also bring about positive physiological changes in us if used correctly.

Where Did Mantras Originate?

Mantras originated from traditions of the Vedic period. This is the period during which the oldest sacred texts of the Indo-Aryans, called Vedas, were being composed (believed to be around the 2nd and 1st millennia BCE continuing up to the 6th century BCE). The Vedas were written in Sanskrit, one of the classical languages of India. As hymns, the mantras constitute the ritual section of the Vedas and are classified according to their meters:Gayatri - twenty-four syllables with nine subdivisions. Ushnik- twenty-eight syllables with seven subdivisions. Prakruti - forty syllables with eight subdivisions. Brhauti - thirty-six syllables with nine subdivisions. Trishtup - forty-four syllables with ten subdivisions. Jagati - forty-eight syllables with three subdivisions. Ajagati - fifty-two syllables.

Shakvari - fifty-six syllables.

Atishakvari - sixty syllables.

Ashti - sixty-four syllables.

Dhruti - seventy-two syllables.

Atidhruti - seventy-six syllables.

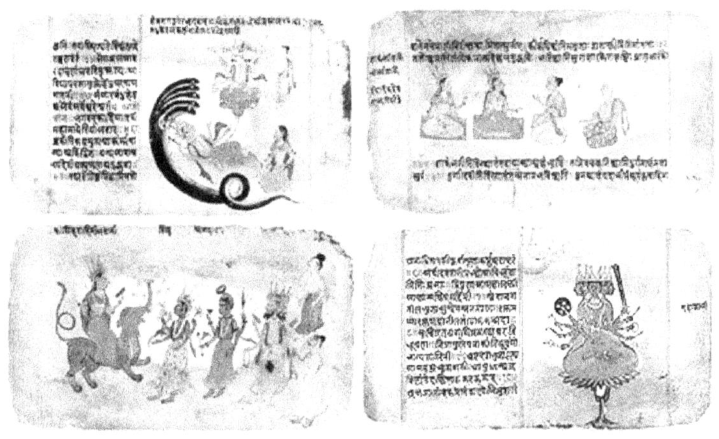

The letters of the Sanskrit alphabet are the elements from which all mantras of Sanskrit origin were derived. It is said that each letter serves as a vehicle of a basic eternal power. When these letters are assembled to form a mantra, they contribute their specific influence to the total effect that becomes the objective of the mantra.

To give an analogy, just think about how individual chemical elements contribute their specific properties to the compounds that are derived from them. Water, for example, contains both of the chemical properties of oxygen and hydrogen.

There are 53 letters of the Vedic Sanskrit alphabet, and therefore, there are 53 basic elemental powers that are available for producing all kinds of effects. Through the agency of mantras, these basic elemental powers can be used in various permutations and combinations.

Here let us take one example of Gayatri Mantra which is if repeatedly meditated produce the results as depicted in following picture.

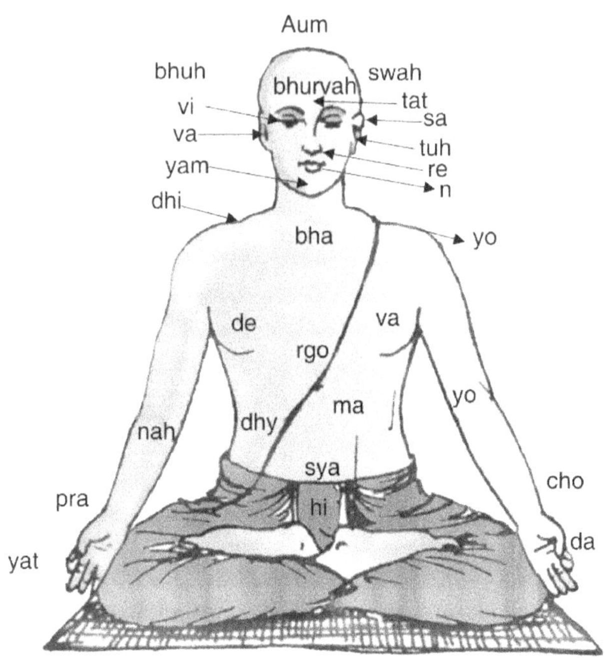

Silently thinking, speaking or chanting the Gayatri mantra influences the physical body, clears the emotional body, leading one to the inner heart. Chanting this mantra or listening to it purifies your body and mind.

ॐ भूर्भुव: स्व: ॐ तत्सवितुर्वरेण्यं
भर्गो देवस्य धीमहि धियो यो न: प्रचोदयात् ।

Om Bhurbhuvah svah Om tatsviturvarenyam
bhargo Devasy Dhimahi Dhiyo yo nah pracho dayat

These Mantras are to be meditated upon in a specific manner to obtain physical and mental powers for which they are meant for. If Japa or Sadhana (meditation) is more on the given rules (*niyam*) they produce the intended results of acquiring specific powers called Siddhis. In our mode of scientific inquiry they result in producing and making subtle changes in one's DNA getting relief from certain discomforts , physical and mental that is certain deceases in our present life and improvement for posterity. Here we are continuing with our example of Gayatri Mantra to high light the procedure prescribed for its meditation. Here we are considering the Chanda (hymans) used for worship is the 'Gayatri' and it is called the Gayatri mantra. The patron God too is Gayatri. The three letters of the divine cosmic word 'OM' are A,U, M are the Bija (seed or root) used for the worship of the cosmic authority, the 'Shakti' (power, potential, energy, viatality,) and the 'Kilaka' (portion) of this 'Vidya', that is knowledge of metaphysics. This mantra is all important as it is worshiped for elimination of hunger and other torments . Gayatri is also called 'Savitri' and is most powerful and strong; She is the bestower of four fruits of manly efforts. They are

intended results of acquiring specific powers called *Siddhis*. In our mode of scientific inquiry they result in producing and making subtle changes in one's DNA getting relief from certain discomforts , physical and mental that is certain deceases in our present life and improvement for posterity. Here we are continuing with our example of Gayatri Mantra to high light the procedure prescribed for its meditation. Here we are considering the Chanda (hymans) used for worship is the 'Gayatri' and it is called the Gayatri mantra. The patron God too is Gayatri. The three letters of the divine cosmic word 'OM' are A,U, M are the Bija (seed or root) used for the worship of the cosmic authority, the 'Shakti' (power, potential, energy, viatality,) and the 'Kilaka' (portion) of this 'Vidya', that is knowledge of metaphysics. This mantra is all important as it is worshiped for elimination of hunger and other torments . Gayatri is also called 'Savitri' and is most powerful and strong; She is the bestower of four fruits of manly efforts. They are

   (i) **Artha** - material prosperity,
   (ii) **Dharana** - righteousness, integrity and honesty,
   (iii) **Kama**- fulfilment of worldly desire and
   (iv) **Moksha** – emancipation and salvation.

Before actually starting your meditation it is advised that the various part of the body are to be cleaned by invoking following Mantras.

   (I) Om Klim hrudyay Namah (ॐ क्लीं हृदयाय नमः)
   (ii) Om Klim Shirase Svah (ॐ क्लीं शिरसे स्वाहा)
   (iii) Om Klim Shikhay Vashat (ॐ क्लीं शिखाय वषट)
   (iv) Om Klim Astray Phat (ॐ क्लीं अस्त्राय फट)

These Mantras are used to sanctify the various points in body before the actual chanting of Gayatri Mantra in your meditation starts.

| Here we must remember, as seen earlier, that both according to Modern Science and vedantic principles are the reality is that astral as well as material world is based on language code originated from genetic code in the form of DNA i.e. Double helix. This language code according to Vedic principles are various sounds emerged from eternal cosmic vibration that is Brahma Nad. 53 Alphabets and wovels of Sanskrit language are emerged from the primordial cosmic sound vibrations to form various life forms, organic and inorganic. Hence different Mantras which are specific sound formations when meditated upon produce

desired result in changing your life's code that is DNA and help in getting some relief from deformities in your DNA changing them for relief in your present life and for posterity. J

Now let us focus on integrated thought processes. Once we accept that the cosmic mind or the 'God principle' forms the basic building block in all entities understanding becomes easy. The same thought is repeated over and over in different contexts to reinforce the operating principles in memory and also to establish their relevance from different planes of view. Each being is with unique cosmic imprints. DNA-double helix). Man and woman are complementary to each other. Embryo logical and neural anatomical studies support the existence of complementary differences between males and females. One's innate nature normally replicates only the data of a part of the primordial matter encoded as his DNA that may undergo modifications/mutations over time. However, all are empowered to enliven even the entire cosmic genome of the holistic consciousness when in resonance with the universal rhythm.

1. DNA: Energy Transfers: Energy Transfers are based on

'complementary pair' functioning of 'cosmic rhythm' cycles, 'universal rhythm' cycles, 'cause/effect' cycles, 'transformation' cycles, 'growth/decay' cycles, 'karmic energy' cycles, and 'autonomous control' cycles.

2. PRANIC ENERGY CONTROL this relates to meditation.

Desire propels the evolutionary activities by acting as a catalyst in requisite energy release from matter. Desire is synonymous with antimatter that causes the release of energy when it annihilates with the matter. A portion of the absolute mass radiated as its aberrations, for carrying out its desire with various I-Ness identities, (Ahankar phenomenon) through pervading and enlivening vitalities in evolution

-        creation - mode and to ultimately converge after the exhaustion of all their karmic energy contents, in the attraction mode at its base -cosmic merger

-        and then to bounce them again due to their own momentum after self-healing in its coherence, thereby completing a cosmic cycle.

This primary transfer cycle generates self-sustaining coherent radiations - energy bursts - energy transfers - that govern and enliven the universal rhythm by its all-knowing integral gender vitality. There is a progressive deterioration in vitality energy level of the released aberrations while there is an increase in their mass coherence during the

cosmic cycle, starting with energy saturation and culminating in energy depletion. In this back drop, the released matter, non-sentient and those of which that undergo evolution changes to become sentient, engage in self-sustaining energy vibrations and motions depending on the vitality of their individual energy/mass contents, big and small, exerting influence on each other through their energy vibrations. Different vibrations emanating as per encoded imprints from different entities represent different aspects of divinity - supra human form, and so have 'material and spiritual implications' in the environment.

Universe is thus a spiritual arena - the domain of 'desire based' consciousness, of all the released matters with energy contents self-sustaining in the gaps of space as Varna and Guna vibrations forming part as the harmonics of the universal rhythm which is sustained by the cosmic forces of singularity.

However the autonomous non-radial, non-rhythmic karmic energy transfers of the ego based complementary pairs interfere with other energy transfers upsetting their 'mass/energy/space horizon' relationships and hence these relationships eventually may cease to exist. The consequent dissociation of energy from these space horizons results in the formation of antimatter. This desire based antimatter annihilates with the remaining pure matter to form fresh 'energy/mass pairs' (DNA), encased in their new compatible space horizons, with compatible orientations and vibrations, according to the environmental contingencies ending in transformations.

These form the basis for perpetuation of the 'many' aspect of the cosmic desire for self-expression. 'Desire' accounts for the spontaneous release of mass and energy unions from all matters to enable ready transformations /transmigrations, as and when the mass/ energy /space relationships of matters get upset. These matters, being only partially invincible, are only transient in nature as they undergo ready transformations. Non sentient matter's identity is sustained by its self-consciousness - immanent - and the holistic consciousness of nature, both making a complement pair of consciousness. Its existence is governed by nature. During the evolutionary progress when its mass becomes coherent to become a sentient matter - astral mass with autonomous self-consciousness that can support the growth/decay cycle of its own mass using it as a medium for experiencing desire gratifications, it becomes a soul-atma (holistic consciousness). That means its body mass becomes a medium for its desire/karmic gratifications.

The autonomous nature of its energy transfers i.e. will power of its self-consciousness (soul) or the collective consciousness of the 'environment'- may even upset their 'mass/energy/space horizon' relationship. This leads to their mass/energy/space collapse leading to release of from its horizon. The body mass becomes inert - death occurs to the being . The astral mass' - self-consciousness - detaches from the body mass union and seeks, because of lingering cosmic desire, a new compatible medium for growth/decay karmic gratifications. and finds a compatible womb for transmigration to maintain compatible karmic continuity of the soul. A human being (a union of varna and enlivening vitality), is a sentient mass - an enlivened non sentient mass that has during the course of its evolution progress acquired the self-actualizing imprints with which it can enliven and support its own growth/decay cycles with sex identities. In a being the karmic energy rises from the base -mooladhara - , the seat of energy attraction, through the spine - human vision axis - self healed by the body mass coherence in tranquility during its passage to the head, before projection into space around for exploration. This repetitive karmic energy dissipation cycles that go on and on according to the encoded data as acts of desire urged by the mind, may end up in upsetting the naturally ordained 'mass/energy/space horizon' relationship ending in the release of energy from this horizon (death of a being).

That means the astral mass gets released from its medium, the body mass, through which it has been savoring karmic gratifications and initiates a new growth/decay cycle through transmigration, according to the lingering vitality of astral mass. Apart from this sequence, the above cycle may also stop abruptly by the external mutations/damage to body DNA. This body mass thereafter undergoes transformation as a non-sentient mass. With this body matter decay, the detached astral mass with unfulfilled karmic desire (mind/ desire/ 1-ness /self-actualization vitality imprints etc.), gets naturally attracted to the cosmic gender enlivening vitality of nature for nature's karmic perpetuation in the environment or to a reproduction cell of male/female union - a womb from where the complementary attitudes and tendencies are derived by the transmigrating soul's self-consciousness - to perpetuate a new 'energy/mass' union with its prior orientation. This means fresh birth through transmigration - a new being with its DNA double helix. A fresh growth/decay cycle - a continuation of the previous one - begins from

there. Transformations in non-sentient matters as also transmigrations as degraded/ upgraded beings, including a variety of other possibilities in between, are the inherent activities in nature's replication processes. 'Desire for self-existence' of the source permeates through all the minds of its aberrations, eternally establishing immortality in the universe. Science has established that, the universe is not made of solid stuff but of energy of consciousness as experienced by what one observes, recognizes and savors through his sensory faculties.

Everything in the universe is made up of 'lux on' various types of light, electrons, quarks, sub atomic particles and components of DNA, encased in respective space fields. Mind is not contained in the body; rather the body is contained in the mind, the reservoir of thoughts - its space field. The body and mind are not separate from each other. We become more aware of what is happening to our lives by steering away from strictly material goals and then we gain more insight into the mind. Mind control techniques aid co-creation activities in all fields of activity.

Non-sentient matter.

It exists as 'mass/energy' bundle with its unique space envelope -aspect of mind - and dormant immanent consciousness. Its DNA double helix comprises one strand of immanent consciousness that sustains the identity of its space envelope and the other, the holistic consciousness of nature's vitality that sustains its 'mass/ energy' make up. It is a non-sentient matter with unique 1-ness imprints etc. whose self-consciousness is autonomous that sustains both its space envelope and also its DNA

[Here we must note that through our concentrated desire while meditating one must take care not to concentrate on worldly benefits but concentrate on desire to get free from this mundane world's pleasures if we want to attain jeevan mukti. For that we will return to our discussion of jeevan mukti as described especially well in Nadbindupanishad.]

सर्वचिन्तां समुत्सृज्य सर्वचेष्टाविवर्जितः ।
नादमेवानुसंध्यान्नादे चित्तं विलीयते ।।४१।।

Sarvachintam samutsrujya sarvacheshtavivarjitah / nadmevanuasandhyannade chittam viliyate /141 II

The aspirant for moksha should consciously forsake all worries, divert

his mind away from all worldly activities and interactions and concentrate upon the 'Nada' , think and contemplate on it so that he can easily submerge his mind, drench in the primordial Sound 'Nada'(i.e. OM) and

fully dissolve it in the latter.

[Here please remember the basic primary proposition agreed by both Modern science and vedant that living world is manifestation of basic language code emrged from sounds emerging from Brahma NAO (OM)]

मकरन्दं पिबन्भृङ्गो गन्धात्रापेक्षते यथा ।
नादासक्तं सदा चित्तं विषयं न हि कान्क्षति ।।४२।।

Makarandam pibanbhrungo gandhatrapexate /

nadasktam sada chittam vishayam n hi kanxati // 42//

Bee does not get attracted by the fragrance of the flower while

drinking its nectar. Similarly the mind which totally engrossed in seeking and hearing the cosmic sound has no inclination to pay attention to pay heed to any sensory perceptions pertaining to gratification to sense organs. It also has no attraction of allurements offered by the objects of the materialistic world and has full concentration in hearing cosmic NAO (OM).

विस्मृत्य विश्वमेकाग्रः कुत्रचिन्न हि धावति ।

मनोमत्तगजेन्द्रस्य विषयोद्यानचारिणः ।।४४।।

Vismrutya vishvamekaayah kutrachinna hi dhavati /
manomattgajendrasya vishayodyancharinah/ /44/ /

Nadbindupanishad

As a result of this concentration , the mind forgets about the external world and its misleading charms, becomes stable and focused and stops wandering recklessly amongst the objects of the world. This mind is compared here with intoxicated wild elephant in the forest and different objects in the world as trees in the forest.

अन्तरङ्गसमुद्रस्य रोधे वेलायतेऽपि वा ।

ब्रह्मप्रणवसंलग्ननादो ज्योतिर्मयात्मकः ।।४६।।

Antarangsmudrasya rodhe velayatepi va /
brahmpravanavsanlagnnado jyotirmayaatmakah 1/46//

Ndabindupanishad

The Nada here acts like dyke or dam to stop the swift waves of the mind which symbolizes its swift and ever-changing fickle nature. Here it is a categorical example of how the specific deep concentration on Nada helps in yogic stance fixing the mind for an intended result, here namely preparing onceself to reach jeevan mukti. It must be remembered that Nada which is associated with the Supreme Brahma is equally self-illuminated and scintillating, radiant and glorious *(ज्योतिर्मय)*.

सशब्दश्चाक्षरे क्षीणे निःशब्दं परमं पदम् ।
सदा नादानुसंधानात्संक्षीणा वासना तु या ।।४९।।

Sashabdshchaxre xinam niahshabdam paramam padam |
sada nadanusandhatsanxina vasana tu ya ||49||

Nadbinduupanishad

When different constituent sounds of the Nada Brahma, that is syllables and vowels which constitute the divine cosmic sound Nada (OM) (please see the discussion of verses 5-14 on page 78 above) merge with each other and collapse back into their point of origin that state is called the soundless supreme state of existence marked by absolute silence. Remember the constant contemplation and meditation upon Nada results in gradual dissipation of all of the worldly desires and yearnings pertaining to gratification of the sense organs. Also seeking of pleasure from the material objects of the world is vanished too. This goes on till the ultimate end which is they completely vanish and cease to have any relevance.

निरञ्जने विलीयते मनोवायू न संशयः ।
नादकोटिसहस्राणि बिन्दुकोटिशतानि च ।।५०।।

Niranjane viliyate mnovayu n sanshyah|
nadkotishtrani bindukotishatani ch||50|| *Nadbindupanishad*

After the different constituent sound vanish both mind and the vital wind force called 'Prana' merge into one another and become one with the supreme, eternal, atributeless, divine, holy, pure and transidental *(niranjana)* entity called Brahma. Thousands of sounds and millions of spots or nodes plung themselves and vanish into that cosmic 'Nada' which is also called 'Pranava' and which is synonymous with Brahma.

With achieving this state seeker gets a status of person freed from bondage of this world's physical bondage and lead the path of tranquility and sublime bliss which is denoted as Sat-Chit-Anand.

Here we must take a note that almost all the major Upanishads describe in a different perspectives that one's goal should be to achieve sadgati and getting relieved from the birth death cycle. No doubt very noble aim. But what happens while a person is still alive and leading life in this world. It is here this thesis tries to find out how much relief one can get from meditation and to what extent. Up till now we had achieved some result in this aspect as our previous discussion would tell you.

Now let us move again to the topic of concept DNA and its co relation to vedant.

As we have seen above DNA is encoded with four interchangeable 'building blocks'. If one chooses to explore on his own through his autonomous energy transfers, he can change the course of his evolution progress by his free will through meditation, but this again can happens only in the back drop of the cosmic contingencies in the universe. As we had seen there are 4 blocks', called 'bases', which can be abbreviated A, T, C, and G; each base 'pairs up' with only one other base: A+ T, T +A, C+G and G+C; that is, an 'A' on one strand of double-stranded DNA with opposing strands, will 'mate' properly only with a 'T' on the other, complementary strand. Replication is performed by splitting (unzipping) the double strand down the middle via relatively trivial chemical reactions, and recreating the 'other half' of each new single strand by drowning each half in a 'soup' made of the four bases.

The concept of formations of new double helix pairs with A+ T, T +A, C+ G has been the basis of life formation where one of the components remains constant while the other component is replaced. Thus innumerable basic pairs are formed rather manifested by sub particles from the vibrations of the eternal cosmic sound called Nad Brahma. This we have already seen in our discussion in the previous paragraphs.

This concept of formation of basic pairs with one component remaining constant while other changing for creation of variety of forms of lives, organic and inorganic was noted in the One of the Upanishad called Savitryupanishad which explains this idea as follows:-

कः सविता का सावित्रीअग्निरेव सविता पृथ्वी सावित्री स यत्राग्निस्तत्पृथ्वि यत्र वै पृथ्वी तत्राग्निस्ते द्वे योनिः तदेकं मिथुनम् ।।१।।

Kah savitaka savitri agnirev savita puthvi savitri sa yatragnistatpruthviyatra vai pruthvi tatragniste dve yoni

tadekam mithunam/11 II   savitritrupanishd

Who is Savita and who is Savitri? Agni (fire) is Savita, Savitri is earth. Where there is fire there is earth and vice versa. They form a couple and by their mutual acquiescence and union the world is produced. Both of them form an interacting and conjugal relationship. They complement and supplement each other. (1). (Here Savita is Sun. Savitri is mother of Vedas called Gayitri: Saraswati: the Goddess of speech and learning. The fire is metaphor for warmth and heat. It is obvious that creation can not exist on earth if the earth frigid and cold.

कः सविता का सावित्री वरुण एव सविताऽऽपः सावित्री स यत्र वरुणस्तदापो यत्र वा आपस्तद्वरुणस्ते द्वे योनिः तदेकं मिथुनं ।।२।।

Kah savita ka savitri varuna eva savita pah savitri sa yatra varunastadapo yatra va aapastdvarunste dve yonih tadekam mithunam ||2|| *Savituopanishad ||2||*

Who is Savita and who is Savitri? Varuna is Savita and water is Savitri. Where there is Varuna there is water and vice-a versa. Both of them form a couple to create the part of the world. They complement and supplement each other.

कः सविता का सावित्री वायुरेव सविताकाशः सावित्री स यत्र वायुस्तदाकाशो यत्र वा आकाशस्तद्वायुस्ते द्वेयोनिस्तदेकं मिथुनं ।।३।।

Kah savita ka savitri vayurev savitakashah savitri s yatra vayustdakasho yatra va akashstdvayuste dve yonistdekm||3||
                    Savitriupanishad

Who is Savita and who is Savitri? Vayu (wind) is Savita and the sky is Savitri. Where there is wind there is sky/space and vice –versa. They are inseparable couple responsible for creating the Part of this world by their union. They complement each other.

कः सविता का सावित्री पुरुष एव सविता स्त्री सावित्री स यत्र पुरुषस्तत्स्त्री यत्र वा स्त्री स पुरुषस्ते द्वे योनिस्तदेकं मिथुनं ।।९।।

Kah Savita ka Savitri purush eav Savita stri Savitri sa yatra purushsttstri yatra va stri purushaste dve yonistdekam mithunam ||9||
                    savitriupanishad

Who is Savita and who is Savitri? The male is Savita and female is Savitri. Where there is a male there is a female and vice-versa. They form conjugal relationship and their union creates the world (individual life-jiva).

Continuing our discussion on the formation of new DNA we can assume that transmigration of beings as a process where the departing soul finds it's complementary through the principle of quantum entanglement, as follows:-

Nature enables the manipulation of the DNA of a reproduction cell by the vibrations of the transmigrating astral mass to attain cosmic potentials (right environmental conditions prevailing). When transcendence of these vibrations to the cosmic horizon is achieved, human beings attain invincibility. With such potentials, beings can experience happiness in bliss. Bliss - resonance with the universal rhythm can be attained even instantly, if right conditions for orientation and coherent self will prevail. Once realized, it need not stay i.e. the period in which their vibration harmonics cross over with the universal rhythm in close proximity is an essential prerequisite for lasting happiness. 'Not possessing ego' is a virtue, but at the same time, the intensive thought being 'conscious of not possessing ego' itself, hinders harmony and also coherence. This awareness enables one to sail in the realm of the universal rhythm without anxieties and to be in blissful harmony in the domain of the universe can be approached and established by the beings by adherence to their innate traits.

Karmic actions against Nature's Harmony and Coherence are sins and those in favor, are virtues and hence conducive to bliss. Swabhavic and Swadharmic actions, being devoid of sins lead to salvation. By coexisting as peeling, to implant its own active DNA strand - self-consciousness - in a compatible reproduction cell of a womb which is a reservoir of holistic consciousness of similar karmic traits, from where it derives its complementary strand - passive strand - to become a sentient complementary double helix pair, a being. If of course the astral mass were to be in tune with the universal rhythm itself and with a right orientation at the moment of its dissociation from the body mass on death, its natural merger can easily take place with the universal rhythm, the invincible vitality (holistic consciousness), integral gender union of the cosmos itself attain liberation.

There is then no re-birth. Replication, procreation, reproduction, co-creation are the normal modes in growth cycles of persons. Transmigration -higher order replication - goes through human male/ female reproduction cells.

Transmigration cycle in beings is synonymous with the cosmic transfer cycle where the cosmic desire vitality enlivens the fertilized seed that grows into the tree of universe and on its ultimate culmination initiates a new cycle. In transmigration of beings the departing soul -

astral mass with immanent vitality - enlivens a reproduction cell of male/female union and using it as a medium grows into a being and on its decay its astral mass with its lingering vitality initiates its entry into a compatible reproduction cell of a male/female sex union, to carry on its lingering karma in a fresh growth/decay cycle.

The lingering karmic desire in the astral mass of sentient being likewise acts as the basis for its transmigration through a compatible womb. It is through these transformations and transmigrations, the Varna and Guna vibrations of the aberrations perpetuate the supra human form in variations Yuga after Yuga, (e.g. year after year) as acts of 'cause and effect' contingencies i.e. one energy transfer influencing the other's vitality in the environment. It is the desire vibrations of the astral mass on death that enables the process of unzipping the DNA double helix of the fertilized male/female reproduction cell to form its complementary strand and become a compatible double helix.

This double helix initiated by the astral mass becomes a fresh life/ being encoded with the tendencies prevailing at the instant of its transmigration that further goes through its growth/decay cycle using its mass as its medium nurtured by both the self-consciousness of the astral mass as well as the holistic consciousness as a complementary pair.

Apart from the nature's common gender vitality - pervading holistic consciousness - used for transmigration of low order sentient matters, the nature's mutually attracting forces of mooladhara of opposite genders of higher order beings provide the holistic vitality to the reproduction cells for enabling enriched transmigrations.

Transformations in non-sentient matter and replication / recreation / reproduction / procreation/ transmigration I co creation etc. in sentient matter are natural processes that are sustained by the cosmic fields of the universe, to carry forward the urge of 'cosmic desire' for 'self-existence as many' to 'explore newer horizons'. In fact by being in resonance with the universal rhythm during their gender union, the human beings can enrich the reproduction cells with optimum cosmic genome enabling the astral masses to go through refined transmigration. Ironically sentient beings merely dissipate the cosmic energy only in sensory pleasures during

gender union, denying nature its chance to play its natural role to enrich the reproduction cells as reservoirs of cosmic genome for optimum evolutionary progress, thus only passing on degradation to posterity.

Apart from this, a being has to strive to upgrade its mass through self-realization to enable its astral mass on death to be in a harmonious orientation with the universal rhythm at the instant of transmigration in to a reproduction cell. Proper orientation and rhythm of the complementary pairs undergoing transmigration i.e. spiritual orientation at the time of death, ensures enriching human species and as its consequence the social up gradation life after life.

Thoughts associated with the Absolute at the time of death are conducive for 'refined transmigration' or even 'liberation' that is merger with the radiance of the absolute Brahman. When the self-consciousness of a being gets into, through the will power of mind, a proper energy rhythm merges with the universal energy rhythm, before all of the energy content of its 'energy/mass' union is exhausted'.

To be a co-creator and be in Bliss, you have to be aware of your nature and also be part of nature's processes. Energy vibrations that emanate from cosmic radiations have spiritual and social relevance. By orienting the mind with the quality of the 'silent witness' i.e. dispassion -thoughts rid of feelings - the human cells can be streamlined and brought in resonance with the universal rhythm for worldly bliss and even with that of the cosmos for invincibility.

This resonance transcending the zone of the universe to that of the cosmos, assure immense cosmic possibilities to human efforts. These autonomous self-referral vibrant potency of the human energy transfers, rising from moo/adhara, the seat of attraction through the spine to the head, the seat of emission for projection into space can through coherence of will power be made to resonate with the universal rhythm.

A good mind controller is a good cosmic energy controller as against a good mind arrester. The universe is an abode of cosmic aberrations. These are desire propelled by their origin. The cosmic nucleus on the contrary is an embodiment of invincible dispassion and hence naturally there is an innate desire in all the beings with different Varna and thus the Guna vibrations for knowing, feeling and ultimately for being the source itself. The evolution culminates with the source itself ultimately. Because faculties namely intelligence, empathy and self-realization respectively

with self-willed dispassion occur with individual's effort through concentrated deep meditation. This has a effect of acquiring knowledge which provides clarity, empathy its true meaning and self-realization that is the spiritual awareness.

Each path leads one to bliss with its own merit and so there are various ways to realize worldly bliss. Environment and will power play a vital role in influencing auto replicating Guna vibrations to adhere to the universal rhythm. Dispassionate will power of course holds the key. All Varna and Guna vibrations if conditioned to be in unison with the universal rhythm can attain the glow-tejas.

Varna is not at all an impediment to invincibility and a factor in attainment of bliss. Varna of course adds colors and shades to the panorama.

All are equally exposed to the cosmic radiations that enliven the universal rhythm and its harmonics. That is all, what equality is about. Self-will alone holds the key to one's invincibility. The oscillating universe' functioning with a precise order shows that the cosmic forces exercise predetermined overall controls over the transformations and transmigrations of the revealed matter, which implies that no fresh matter/energy inputs are ruled out during one cosmic cycle. This destiny carries on in eternal cycles.

Coming to our main thesis let us turn to hypothesis that it is possible through individual will power properly oriented through Yogic Sadhana one can achieve relief from present impediments, such as deceases besides achieving principle goal of getting moksha.

Jabalodarshan Upanishad is a dialogue between the Lord Dattatreya (An incarnation of Lord Vishnu) and his disciple Samkriti. Lord Dattatreya explains the various Asanas (yogic stance) and their purpose and how they are helpful in obtaining Moksha that is salvation and relief from deceases in person's present life. We will consider here in brief the teachings of Lord Dattatreya in plane language while omitting the dialogues between him and his disciple.

Here we are considering only those slokas which directly refer to the relief from deceases and are relevant to our discussion on how changes in our DNA that is genetic code can be achieved through invoking powers through deep meditation.

सांकृते श्रुणु वक्ष्यामि योगं साष्टाङ्‌दर्शनम्।
यमश्च नियमश्चैव तथैवासवनमेव च ।।४।।

प्राणायस्तथा ब्रह्मन्प्रत्याहारसततः परम्।
धारणा च तथा ध्यानं समाधिश्चाष्टमं मुने ।।५।।

अहिंसा सत्यमस्तेयं ब्रह्मचर्यं दयार्जवम्।
क्षमा धृतिर्मिताहारः शौचं चैव यमा दश ।।६।।

जाबलोदर्षन उपनिषद खण्ड ।।१।।

Sankrute srunu vaxyami yogam sashtangdarshanam / yamashch niyameaishch tathaivasvnmeva ch 1/41/ pranaysttha brahmnpratyaharsattah param /

dharana ch tatha dhyanam samadhishchashtamam mune 1/51/ ahinsa satyamsteyam brahmcharyam dyaarjanam /

xama dhrutirmitaharah shoucham chaiv yama dash 1/61/

The system of philosophy of yoga has eight main branches or limbs. They are –

(i)   Varna (self-restraint of passion),

(ii)   Niyama (following rules and regulations; a regulated life; sacrosanct principles and tenets, codes of conduct),

(iii)   Asanas (various sitting positions) ,

(iv)   Pranayama (control of breath),

(v)   Pratyahara (to divert the mind away from gratification of sense organs and exercising control over it),

(vi)   Dharana (firm belief, conviction and faith),

(vii)   Dhyana (concentration and focusing of the mind and intellect, contemplation and meditation), and finally

(viii)   Samadhi (a trance like state when the ascetic loses all awareness of the external world and remains in a blissful state).

Varna (self-restraint) also has ten types and they are,

(i)   Ahinsa (non-violence and non-cruelty),

(ii)   Satya (truthfulness),

(iii)   Asteya (non-theft or non-stilling),

(iv)   Brahmacharya (celibacy, abstinence, continence, non-lust),

(v)   Daya (mercy, compassion),

(vi)   Xama (forgiveness),

(vii)   Saralata (simplicity, humility, non-deceit),

(viii)   Dhruti (stability, unwavering and steadfastness of mind),

(ix)   Mitahara (regulated diet), and

(x)   Shouch (purity, both external and internal).

Here we have outlined the basic tenets or methods that one has to follow while undertaking Yoga Sadhana. Cantos (chapters) 3 to 10 of this Upanishad deal with Yoga rather that is the main purpose of the Lord Dattatreya to enlighten us the importance of Yoga Sadhana.

Here we are not going to dwell upon the entire gambit of this Upanishad as that is not the subject matter of our enquiry, but only highlighting those slokas wherein Lord Dattatreya had mentioned about utilizing the Yoga Sadhana for amelioration of individual Jiva's present life while desiring for Jivan mukti. Here it is cleared that as against the general belief that Yoga is to be followed for one's emancipation and liberation from the obligations of mundane environment of this artificial world but also to get relief from the diseases and impediments faced by person in his present life.

Canto 3 of this jabaloupanishad deals with Yoga. This describes the various 'Asanas' or sitting positions during Yoga exercises. We here are touching only those slokas which mention that the exercises relieve a person from various kinds of deceases. In another words they help in making changes in your DNA code for present life and for recording information in the genetic code for posterity. Because our inquiry here is restricted to our hypothesis of how the cosmic mind with the help of individual mind-soul can effect changes in DNA and not the full discourse on Yoga Sadhana which is entirely a different subject.

स्वस्तिकं गोमुखं पद्मं विरसिंहासने तथा ।
भद्रं मुक्तासनं चैव मयुरासनमेव च ॥१॥
सुखसनसमाख्यं च नवमं मुनिपुङ्गव ।
जानुर्वोरन्तरे कृत्वा सम्यक् पादतले उभ ॥२॥
समग्रिवशिरःकायः स्वस्तिकं नित्यमभ्यसेत् ।
सव्ये दक्षिणगुल्फं तु पृष्ठपाश्रेव नियोजयेत ॥३॥
दक्षिणेऽपि तथा सयं गोमुखं तत्प्रचक्षते ।
अङ्गुष्ठावधी गृहिणीयादधस्ताभ्यां व्युत्क्रमेण तु ॥४॥
ऊवीरुपरि विपेन्द्र कृत्वा पादतलद्वयम् ।
पद्मासनं भवेत्प्राज्ञ सर्वरोगभयापहम् ॥५॥

Swastikam gomukam padam virasinhasane tatha /

bhadram muktasanam chaiv murasanev ch II 1 II sukhasanmakham ch navam munipungava/

janurvorntare krutva samyak padtale ubhe 11211 samagrivshirahkayah swastika nityambhyaset /

Savye daxinnepi ttha sayam gomukham tatprachxate /

angshthavdhi gruhiniyaddhstabhyam vyutkramen tu 11411 urvorupari vipendra krutva padtaldvayam /

padmasanam bhavetpradnya sravarogabhayapham IISII

Asanas (various sitting positions) are nine kinds:-

(i) Swastika, (ii) Gomulka,(iii) Padmasana, (iv) Virasana,

(v) Sinhasana,(vi) Bhadrasana, (vii) Muktasana, (viii) Mayurasana,(ix) Skuhasana.

To sit crossed legged so that the foot of one leg rests on the middle of the thigh of the other side between knee joint and pelvic girdle, with the sole pointing outwards, while keeping the chin , the head and the body straight (in a vertical straight line position) is called 'Swastika Asana". This sitting posture should be practiced daily. To bend the right leg at the knee joint and tuck the ankle of the right foot under the base of the thigh of the left leg below the buttocks of that side (and the ankle of joint of the left under the base of the right thigh below the right buttocks) is called 'Gomukh Asana'.

This is how the cow sits. While sitting in this posture first leg is folded in and tucked below the buttock of the opposite side, while the other leg is stretched out in the front. After sometime, the process is reversed - the stretched out leg is folded in and the folded leg is stretched out. To keep the foot of one leg on the thigh of the apposite leg (i.e. right foot on the left thigh and the left foot on the right thigh), taking each hand behind and round the back to clasp the big toe of the same side placed on the thighs of the corresponding opposite leg (i.e. left hand should clasp the big toe of the left leg, which has been placed on the right thigh and the vice versa) is called Baddha Padmasana or closed padmasana. Lord Dattareya advises here that this Asana removes the fear from all the deceases and has the potential to provide good health.

गुल्फौ तु वृषणस्याधः सीवन्याः पाश्वच्योः क्षिपेत् ।
पाश्र्वपादौ च पाणिभ्यां दृढं बध्वा सुनिश्चलम् ।
भद्रासनं भवेदेतद्विषरोगविनाशनम् ॥८॥

Gulfau tu vrushanasyadhah sivanyaah parshvayoh xipet / parshvapadau ch panibhyam drdham bdhva sunishchalam / bhdrasanam bhvetedvishrogvinashanam I/Bl/

To sit in a posture by placing the two ankle joints under the buttocks on either side of the suture i.e. the junction point of the testicles and the anus such that they (the two ankle joints) touch each other and then using the hands to firmly clasp the soles from the rear side of the buttock, is called Bhadrasana. This posture (meditation in this posture) can neutralize the effects of all diseases which cause the production of toxins in the body, or which are caused by administration of poisons or other toxins in the body. It helps in getting rid of other diseases as well.

In Canto 6 of this Jabalodarshanaupanishd Lord Dattatreya narrates the final stages of benefits of Pranayama in a very succinct manner.

प्राणायामक्रमं वक्ष्ये सांकृते श्रुणु सादरम् ।
प्राणायाम इति प्रोक्तो रेचपुरककुम्भकैः ॥१॥
वर्णत्रयात्मकाः प्रोक्ता रेचपुरककुम्भकाः ।
स एष प्रणवः प्रोक्तः प्राणायामस्तु तन्मयः ॥२॥

Pranayamkramam vaxye sankrute srunu sadaram / pranayama iti prokto rechpurakkumbhakaih 1/11/ varnatrayatmakah prokta rechpurakkukumbhakah / s esh prnavah proktah pranayamstu tanmayah 1/21/

Lord Dattatreya observes "Pranayama has been defined as the control of breath by three steps called (1) 'Purak' (2) 'kumbhak' (3) 'Rechak'. The divine word OM has three syllables or letters (A. U. M) and they are treated as being equivalent to 'Purak', 'Kumbhak' and 'rechak' process respectively. Since these three individual letters or syllables of OM compositely become OM when spoken together and since they are also equivalent to the three steps of 'Pranayama' the latter is also deemed to be symbolic of OM which in turn is synonymous with the cosmic 'NADA' and the Supreme Brahma.'

सर्वरोगविनिर्मुक्तो जिवेद्वर्षशतं नरः ।

नासाग्रधारणाद्वापि जितो भवति सुव्रतः।।२३।।

सर्व्रोगनिवृत्ति स्यान्नाभिमध्ये तु धारणात् ।

शरिरलघुता विप्र पदाङ्गुषठनिरोधनात्।।२४।।

A person practicing Yoga, who always drinks fresh air through his tongue, becomes free from tiredness and fatigue as well as a burning sensation in the body. He always remains decease free. Here Lord Dattatreya advises that the wind should be pulled in through the tongue and held at the gullet. By doing so he gets much needed relief and happiness in his daily endeavor.

In conclusion it is stressed that with the concentrated meditation followed according to precepts of shatras as narrated above it is possible to make changes in our DNA correcting various diseases effecting changes in genetic code of our life and even in death the genetic code that is our double helix can be rearranged for getting free from birth -death cycle or changed to the extent of removing ailments or deformities from them and encoding that information in the code for posterity.

COSMIC MIND, MEDITATION & DNA

Publisher :

Udveli Books, India
udvelibooks@gmail.com

Cover Page: Angad Yadav

E Book creation by Udveli Books, India
First Edition : 28 th July 2023

Notice of Rights